Mexico

BY
MICHAEL KRAMME, Ph.D.

ISBN 1–58037–088–8

Printing No. CD–1323

Mark Twain Media, Inc., Publishers
Distributed by Carson-Dellosa Publishing Company, Inc.

TABLE OF CONTENTS

TIME LINE

B.C.

Before 8000	The first stone-age humans move into the region from the north
2500	Early Mayan culture
1200	Early Olmec culture (Peak of culture 700 to 400)

A.D.

250–900	Mayan culture flourishes
900–1200	Toltec era
1200–1300	Aztec empire expands
1440–1468	Reign of Aztec ruler Montezuma I
1492	Columbus discovers the Americas
1519	Cortés lands
1598	Spanish conquest complete
17th–18th centuries	Spanish colonial rule
1810	Independence proclaimed
1821	Independence achieved
1836	Texas declares independence (battle of the Alamo)
1846–1848	Mexican War (between Mexico and the United States)
1858–1861	Wars between liberals and conservatives
1863	French take over, Maximilian becomes emperor
1867	Juárez defeats Maximilian
1876	Diaz in power
1910	Revolution, 10 years of civil war begins
1958	Women allowed to vote
1968	Summer Olympics held in Mexico

MAP OF MEXICO
United States
San Diego
Tijuana
El Paso
Juárez
Rio Grande River
BAJA CALIFORNIA
GULF OF CALIFORNIA
SIERRA MADRE OCCIDENTAL
MEXICAN PLATEAU
Monterrey
SIERRA MADRE ORIENTAL
GULF OF MEXICO
Mazatlán
PACIFIC OCEAN
Puerto Vallarta
Guadalajara
Lake Chapala
SIERRA MADRE DEL SUR
Mexico City
Puebla
Veracruz
BAY OF CAMPECHE
YUCATAN PENINSULA
Cancún
Cozumel
Belize
Acapulco
ISTHMUS OF TEHUANTEPEC
Guatemala
Honduras
El Salvador

MEXICO: FACTS AT A GLANCE

Official name: The United Mexican States *(Los Estados Unidos Mexicanos)*

Capital: Mexico City

Land area: 762,000 square miles (1,978,000 square kilometers); three times the size of Texas

Borders: United States (north), Guatemala and Belize (south), Gulf of Mexico and Caribbean Sea (east), Pacific Ocean (west)

Highest point: Citlaltépetl (Orizaba Volcano) 18,700 feet

Longest River: Rio Grande 1,300 miles (2,100 kilometers) (not counting the part in the United States)

Population: 88,335,000 (1990)

Largest cities: Mexico City (18,154,000), Guadalajara (2,587,000), Monterrey (2,335,000), Puebla (1,218,000)

Government: Federal republic with two legislative bodies; president is head of state; 31 states

Official language: Spanish

Currency: Peso (one peso equals 100 centavos)

Religion: Roman Catholic 92.6%, Protestant 3.3%, Nonreligious 3.1%, Jewish 0.1%, others 0.9%

Major resources: agriculture and fishing 9.0%, mining 3.9%, manufacturing 26.4%, trade 27.4%, government/defense 14.9%

Industries: chemicals, coffee, cotton, lead, oil, rubber, salt, seafood, steel, sugar, sulfur, textiles, tourism, transportation equipment, vegetables

MEXICO: AN INTRODUCTION

The official name of Mexico is "The United Mexican States." In Spanish, it is *Los Estados Unidos Mexicanos.*

Mexico shares a 1,933-mile border with the United States. To the south, Mexico shares its border with Guatemala and Belize. Its western coast is on the Pacific Ocean, and the eastern coast is on the Gulf of Mexico.

Mexico is the largest Spanish-speaking country in the world. It is the second-largest Roman Catholic nation in the world.

There is colorful diversity in Mexico's culture. The major blend is of Spanish and Indian cultures. Ancient civilizations include the Mayan, Olmec, Toltec, and Aztec Indian cultures. The Spanish conquest began in the sixteenth century and lasted for over 300 years.

Mexico is a nation of contrasts. It has ruins of ancient Indian cities, churches from the Spanish colonial period, and modern skyscrapers.

Many mineral resources are found in Mexico, but there is limited farmland. Major crops include citrus fruits, beans, corn, bananas, pineapple, cotton, coffee, sugar cane, cacao, coca, wheat, oats, and rice.

Mexico has a varied climate and geography. It is a mountainous country with two mountain ranges enclosing a dry plateau. Mexico contains large deserts, beautiful sand beaches, and jungle wetlands.

Mexico has one of the world's fastest growing populations. Some of its people live in great wealth just a few miles from some of the world's largest slums. The unemployment rate continues to grow each year. The population of the Mexico City region is the largest urban area in the world. Mexico City itself (not counting the adjoining area) is the world's third largest city.

In addition to the population problem, increasing pollution, crime, and drug usage and trafficking plague the country.

Despite its problems, Mexico also has many popular tourist sites. In addition to the ancient Indian ruins, thousands of tourists visit Mexico's resort cities. Popular vacation resort destinations include Cancún, Acapulco, Mazatlán, Puerto Vallarta, and Veracruz. These are often stops for cruise ships sailing in the Caribbean or the Pacific Ocean.

Mexico is one of the fastest growing industrial nations on Earth. Major industries include petroleum and tourism. It may have the largest oil pool in the Western Hemisphere. Auto plants and steel mills are increasing production each year.

Mexico is also noted for its colorful fiestas or celebrations. Popular entertainment includes bullfights, soccer games, and rodeos. In addition to national holidays, Mexicans observe most Roman Catholic religious celebrations.

September 16 is Mexico's Independence Day. It celebrates Mexico's 1810 rebellion against Spanish control.

The Mexican culture has a great influence on the United States. Mexican art and music are increasing in popularity. Many Mexican foods such as tacos and enchiladas are more popular than ever.

Name ______________________ Date ______________

Questions for Consideration

1. What is Mexico's official name (in English)?

____

2. What is Mexico's official name (in Spanish)?

____

3. How long is the United States-Mexican border?

____

4.–5. What two countries share Mexico's southern border?

____

____

6.–7. Mexico is a blend of what two major cultures?

____

____

8. What is the world's third largest city?

____

9.–10. What are two of Mexico's major resort cities?

____

____

11.–12. What are two of Mexico's major problems mentioned in the article?

____

____

____

13. Of what resource may Mexico have the largest pool in the Western Hemisphere?

____

14. On what day does Mexico celebrate its independence?

____

Name ______________________________ Date ________________

Which Does Not Belong?

One word in each list below does not belong with the others. Circle the word in each group that is different. Tell why it is different on the line below each word group.

1. Belize	Guatemala	Panama	United States
2. Aztec	Mayan	Olmec	Spanish
3. Acapulco	Cancún	Mexico City	Puerto Vallarta
4. corn	cotton	onions	sugar cane
5. burritos	enchiladas	pizza	tacos

List the Contrasts

Mexico is a land of many contrasts. Give examples of the contrasts mentioned in the introduction article.

1. Cultures:

_____________________ and _____________________

2. Buildings:

_____________________, _____________________, and

____

3. Geography:

_____________________ and _____________________

4. Climate:

_____________________ and _____________________

Name ______________________________ Date ____________________

An Art Project

Look at some pictures of Mexico in a book or encyclopedia to give you some ideas, and then make a travel poster to advertise Mexico.

Matching

Match the items in the first column with the correct response in the second column. Place the correct letters from the second column next to the items in the first column.

_____ 1. Mountains
_____ 2. Cotton
_____ 3. Cancún
_____ 4. Arid
_____ 5. Desert
_____ 6. Oil
_____ 7. Acapulco
_____ 8. San Diego
_____ 9. Wetlands
_____ 10. Coffee
_____ 11. Steel
_____ 12. Plateau
_____ 13. Bananas
_____ 14. Santa Fe
_____ 15. Tourism

A. Mexican resort area
B. Mexican geography
C. Mexican climate
D. Mexican industry
E. Mexican farm product
F. Not Mexican

MEXICO'S GEOGRAPHY

Northern Mexico borders the southwest region of the United States. The Rio Grande River, also known as the Rio Bravo del Norte, forms much of the border. Guatemala and Belize border Mexico on the south. The Gulf of Mexico and the Bay of Campeche border the east, and the Pacific Ocean forms the western border.

Mexico is somewhat triangular or funnel-shaped. It covers an area of over 750,000 square miles. It is about 1,850 miles long from north to south. The width varies from 135 miles to more than 1,200 miles.

There are a variety of land types and climates in Mexico. The climate is Arctic cold near the summits of its mountains, while much of the land is arid desert. Along the coastal areas there are tropical jungles.

Mexico is a mountainous country with three major volcanic mountain ranges, all running north and south. One range is the Sierra Madre Occidental. It is in the northwestern part of the country. The Sierra Madre Oriental is in the east. The Sierra Madre del Sur is in the southwestern region of the country. Mexico's highest mountain is Citlaltépetl, also known as the Orizaba Volcano. It is the third-highest mountain in North America, rising 18,700 feet.

A large plateau, which is more than a mile above sea level, lies in the central region. The plateau is desert in the north, including the area along the border with the United States. The southern part of the plateau contains farmland.

Mexico includes two major peninsulas. The Yucatan Peninsula in the south extends into the Gulf of Mexico. Baja California is a long peninsula on the west, running parallel to the mainland. It is a long, narrow, mountainous land separated from the mainland by the Gulf of California.

For its size, Mexico has few lakes and rivers. Mexico's longest river is the Rio Grande. It begins in the United States, and it then forms the border between the two countries for about 1,300 miles. The Grijalva River, Mexico's second longest, has the largest volume of water. The Lerma River begins west of Mexico City and empties into Lake Chapala. Lake Chapala is the largest natural lake in the country. The Santiago River then flows out of Lake Chapala into the Pacific Ocean.

Mexico is on unstable land. It is on the western edge of the North American tectonic plate, and it is also near the Pacific, Cocos, and Caribbean plates. These tectonic plates are still moving. The interactions of the plates cause many earthquakes and volcanoes. A major earthquake devastated Mexico City in 1985. It killed 20,000 people and destroyed hundreds of buildings.

Name ______________________________ Date ____________________

Questions for Consideration

1. What country borders Mexico on its northern side?

____

2.–3. What two countries border Mexico on its southern side?

____

____

4. What ocean is on Mexico's western side?

____

5.–6. What two bodies of water are on Mexico's eastern coast?

____

____

7. What is Mexico's basic shape?

____

8. What are the first two names of the three major Mexican mountain ranges?

____

9. What is Mexico's highest mountain?

____

10.–11. What are the names of Mexico's two major peninsulas?

____

____

12. What is Mexico's longest river?

____

13. What is the largest natural lake in Mexico?

____

14.–15. What two types of natural disasters often occur in Mexico?

____

____

Name ______________________________ Date ____________________

Map Exercise

Using an atlas to help, locate the following on the map below.

Countries:

BELIZE	GUATEMALA	UNITED STATES

Bodies of Water:

BAY OF CAMPECHE	GULF OF CALIFORNIA	GULF OF MEXICO
LAKE CHAPALA	PACIFIC OCEAN	RIO GRANDE

Mountain Ranges:

SIERRA MADRE OCCIDENTAL	SIERRA MADRE ORIENTAL
SIERRA MADRE DEL SUR	

Land Forms:

BAJA CALIFORNIA	MEXICAN PLATEAU	YUCATAN PENINSULA

Name ______________________________ Date ____________________

Building Your Geography Vocabulary

Some of the geography terms used in the narrative are familiar to you, but others may be new. Using a dictionary, write out the exact meaning of each of the following geographic terms.

1. Bay: ____

____

____

2. Desert: ____

____

____

3. Gulf: ____

____

____

4. Mountain: ____

____

____

5. Peninsula: ____

____

____

6. Plateau: ____

____

____

7. Volcano: ____

____

____

MEXICO'S PEOPLE

Mexico has many ethnic groups. The blend of Spanish and Indian heritage makes for a colorful and lively nation. The many *fiestas* or celebrations include lively music and dance, colorful costumes, and ethnic foods. Many fiestas include bullfighting. Bullfighting is the national sport of Mexico. Soccer is the most popular participation sport, while baseball is increasing in popularity.

Over half of the Mexican people are *mestizos*, which is a mix of European and native Indian. About one-third are native Indians. The rest of the people are from several minority groups.

Mexico has no official religion. However, about 95 percent of the people are Roman Catholic. Just over three percent are Protestant. In addition to their Christian beliefs, many of the Indians still follow traditional beliefs and practices.

The Virgin of Guadalupe is the nation's patron saint. Each year, hundreds of thousands of worshipers make a pilgrimage to her shrine in Mexico City.

The official language of Mexico is Spanish. Mexico is the world's largest Spanish-speaking nation. Mexico has 79 million people who speak Spanish. Spain has only 38 million.

About 3.5 million Mexicans speak *Náhuatl,* the Aztec language spoken before the Spaniards arrived. More than 100,000 people speak about 50 different Indian languages.

Population growth is a major problem in Mexico. The population is growing 50 percent faster than the world average. It is three times as fast as the United States. More than two-thirds of Mexicans live in or around the three largest cities, Mexico City, Guadalajara, and Monterrey. Over one-half of the population is under the age of twenty.

The fast-growing population and the lack of enough good farmland have created rising unemployment. Families in search of work often migrate to the United States.

Mexico is a poor nation. One estimate stated that five percent of the people lived in luxury. Twenty to 30 percent were middle class. More than 60 percent were poor.

The government began a program of adult education to help decrease illiteracy. Today, the government requires all children to attend a six-year free elementary school program. Many students then attend a secondary school or technical school; however, only about five percent of the students attend an institution of higher learning.

Name ______________________________ Date ____________________

Questions for Consideration

1.–2. What are the two major ethnic heritage groups of Mexico?

3. What is the national sport of Mexico?

4. What is a *mestizo?*

5. How many Mexicans are native Indians?

6. What is the largest religious group in Mexico?

7. Who is Mexico's patron saint?

8.–10. What are Mexico's three largest cities?

11. How long are all Mexican children required to attend school?

12. What is the official language of Mexico?

13. What is *Náhuatl?*

14. What percent of Mexico's people are poor?

Name ______________________________ Date ____________________

Understanding Pie Graphs

Mexico's population is over 88,000,000. Mexico's heritage comes from several ethnic groups. The graph at the right shows the percentages of these groups. To answer the following questions, determine what the actual numbers are.

1. About how many Mexicans are *mestizos*?

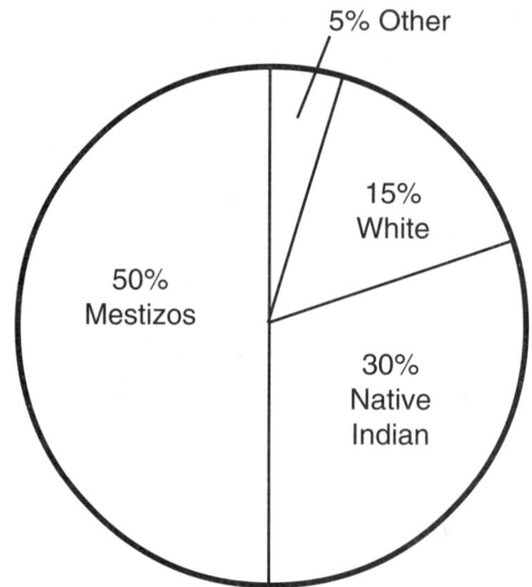

2. About how many Mexicans are native Indians?

____

3. About how many Mexicans are white?

____

4. About how many Mexicans are from other ethnic groups?

____

Mexico's gross national product recently was over $170 billion ($170,000,000,000). The graph at the right shows the approximate percentages of major parts of the economy. To answer the following questions, determine what the actual numbers are.

5. About how many dollars came from trade?

____

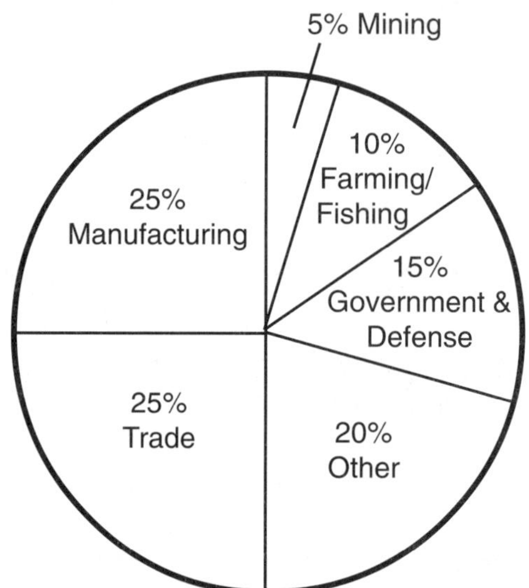

6. About how many dollars came from mining?

____

7. About how many dollars came from manufacturing?

____

8. About how many dollars came from farming and fishing?

____

Name ______________________________ Date ____________________

Crossword Puzzle

Use the clues below to complete the puzzle. You can find the words in the narrative about Mexico's people.

ACROSS

1. Families looking for work often _____ to the United States.
6. The official language of Mexico
7. All Mexican children attend a six-year free _____ school.
8. The national sport of Mexico
10. The most popular participation sport in Mexico
13. Náhuatl is the language of this Indian group.
15. Lack of farmland is one of the causes of this.

DOWN

2. The Virgin of _____ is Mexico's patron saint.
3. The growth rate of this is three times that of the United States.
4. People who have a mix of European and Indian heritage
5. Mexican celebrations
9. Most Mexicans are of this religion (two words).
11. An adult education program was started to help decrease _____.
12. About this many Indian languages are spoken in Mexico.
14. Over one-half of Mexico's population is under this age.

EARLY CIVILIZATIONS

The Olmec civilization left behind artifacts such as these huge heads carved from stone.

Many scientists believe that the first settlers in what is now Mexico arrived from the north. They believe that near the end of the Ice Age (about 8000 B.C.) tribes came from Siberia in what is now Russia into Alaska. They traveled over a piece of land where the Bering Strait is today. This land is now under water. These tribes then continued to migrate south and arrived in Mexico between 2000 and 1000 B.C.

These early Indian tribes were hunters and gatherers. All of their food came from near where they camped. When the food supply ran out, they moved to another area. About 1000 B.C., they discovered agriculture. When they began to plant crops, they could settle in one area more permanently.

These early tribes formed a culture we know today as the Olmec civilization. The Olmecs settled along the central plain of Mexico and the coastal areas of the Gulf of Mexico. The Olmec culture lasted from about 1200 until 100 B.C. The civilization reached its peak from 700 to 400 B.C. The Olmecs influenced many later Indian civilizations.

The Olmec culture evolved into a well-developed civilization. They used a form of picture writing. They had a number system and a calendar. The Olmecs also developed a form of government and religious organization. However, we do not know about the daily lives of the Olmecs or how the civilization ended.

Ruins of two Olmec cities, San Lorenzo and La Venta, still exist. Archeologists found many artifacts from the Olmec era in these cities. The most famous of these were giant heads made of carved stone. The stone heads were discovered in San Lorenzo. These heads are nine feet high and weigh about 40 tons each. The main structure discovered in La Venta was a volcano-shaped pyramid over 110 feet tall.

Scientists believe the Altiplano tribe descended from the Olmecs. The Altiplano civilization flourished from about 200 B.C. until A.D. 600.

The Altiplano built the city of Teotihuacán. It became their capital and covered over eight square miles. The city once had a population of over 100,000 people. Several structures of Teotihuacán remain. It is a popular tourist site today. The most famous structure still standing in Teotihuacán is the Pyramid of the Sun. It is 200 feet tall and as large at its base as the Great Pyramid in Egypt. Other famous structures still standing are the Pyramid of the Moon, the Temple of Quetzalcoatl (the serpent temple), and the Temple of the Jaguars.

The city of Teotihuacán was destroyed and burned in about A.D. 750. Some believe that outside tribes invaded and destroyed the city. Others believe that the Altiplano destroyed their own city.

Just as with the Olmecs, the fate of the Altiplano civilization remains a mystery.

Name ________________________________ Date ____________________

Questions for Consideration

1. When do scientists believe tribes first came from Siberia to Alaska?

2. Where was the land they traveled over to make this early journey?

3. When did these tribes likely arrive in what is now Mexico?

4. What was the name of the culture formed by these early tribes?

5. During what years did this culture reach its peak?

6.–7. Ruins of what two cities of this culture still exist?

8. What now famous items of carved stone were discovered in one of these cities?

9. What was the name of the second major tribe discussed in the narrative?

10. When did this civilization flourish?

11. What was the name of their capital city?

12. What is the most famous structure in this city?

13. In what year was this city destroyed?

14. What happened to both of these famous civilizations?

Name ______________________________ Date ______________

Using a Time Line

This time line gives the important dates of the early civilizations of Mexico. Use it to answer the questions below.

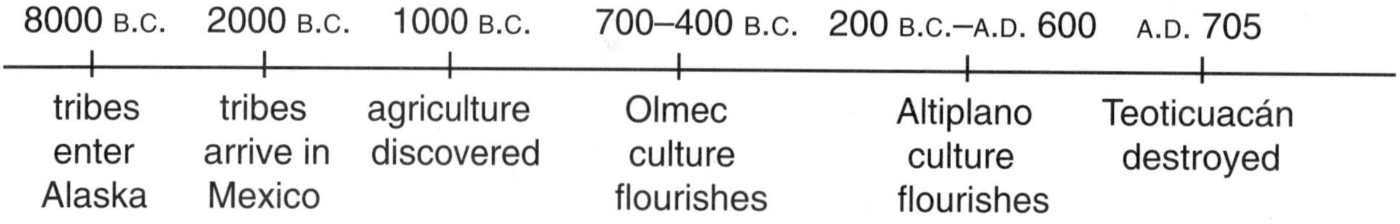

1. How much time passed from when the first tribes entered Alaska until the city of Teotihuacán was destroyed? ______________________________

2. How many years passed from the time the tribes entered Alaska until they entered Mexico? ______________________________

3. How old was agriculture when the peak of the Olmec civilization began? __________

4. How many years passed from the end of the Olmec civilization until the beginning of the peak of the Altiplano culture? ______________________________

5. How long did the Olmec civilization flourish? ______________________________

An Art Project

If you can find pictures of the ruins of the Olmec or Altiplano cultures, make drawings or paintings of major items or ruins from them. Possible subjects might be the ruins of major temples or the famous carved stone heads.

Using your imagination, make a drawing of the center of the city of Teotihuacán.

Name ______________________________ Date ____________________

A Possible Journey

On the map below, draw what you imagine would be the route that the ancient tribes used in their migration to Mexico. Place an **X** where each of the following might have happened and give the possible date for each event.

- The beginning of the migration
- When they entered what is now the United States
- When they reached what is now Mexico
- When Teotihuacán was burned

THE MAYAS

The Mayan culture was one of the most important in the history of Mexico. The early Mayas borrowed from the Olmec culture. The Maya civilization lasted from about 2500 B.C. until the Spanish conquest in the A.D. 1500s. The era of greatest importance for the Mayas lasted from about A.D. 250 to 900.

The Mayas settled in what is now southern Mexico, including the Yucatan Peninsula. They also settled in Honduras, Belize, El Salvador, and Guatemala.

The Mayas built many cities. Most of the cities included large open plazas and ceremonial centers with pyramid-shaped temples.

Tikal, their largest city, may have had a population of 100,000 or more. Tikal is in modern Guatemala. Other major cities located in Mexico include Copán and Chichén Itzá. The Pyramid of Kukulcan with its great staircase is one of the most famous Mayan structures. The ruins of these cities are major tourist attractions today.

The Mayas developed advanced systems of agriculture, including irrigation systems in the dryer areas. In the swamp areas they developed methods of building mounds for growing plants. Maize (corn) became their major crop. They also grew beans, peppers, squashes, tomatoes, avocados, pumpkins, and cacao. The Mayas discovered how to make chocolate out of cacao beans.

They also developed the most advanced system of writing of the ancient Americans. They did not have an alphabet. Instead they used a combination of pictures to represent ideas and symbols to represent sounds. Today, we know of about 800 different Mayan glyphs (picture symbols). The Mayas also developed a method of making paper, and they wrote books. Most of the books are lost, but a few samples remain in museums in Europe.

The Mayas developed systems of mathematics and astronomy. These were more advanced than the systems of the ancient Egyptians, Greeks, or Romans. The Mayas were the first culture to use the idea of a zero. Mayan priests studied the movements of the Sun, Moon, planets, and stars. They could predict eclipses and the orbit of the planet Venus. The great observatory at Chichén Itzá still remains. The Mayas developed a calendar that had 365 days, divided into 18 months of 20 days each.

The Mayan religion had many gods and goddesses. Each year a variety of religious festivals were held. Many of their religious ceremonies included human sacrifice. Each city-state of the empire had its own religious leader. He was called the *halach uinic.* The halach uinic was a living god. He ruled until his death. He dressed in colorful clothes and wore a large headdress.

The end of the great Mayan civilization remains one of the world's greatest mysteries. It was the most important culture in the new world in A.D. 900, but suddenly the Mayas left their cities and scattered throughout the country. We do not know the reason or reasons why the great Mayan civilization ended.

The Mayas continued to farm in the region, however, and Christopher Columbus met some Mayas in 1502. Many Mexicans today are descendents of the Mayas.

Name ______________________ Date ______________

Questions for Consideration

1. From what culture did the Mayas borrow?

2. When did the Mayan culture exist?

3. What peninsula was home to the Mayas?

4.–5. What two cities in Mexico did the Mayas build?

6. What is the most famous Mayan structure?

7. What was the major crop of the Mayas?

8. What are glyphs?

9. What mathematical idea were the Mayas the first to use?

10. How many months did the Mayan calendar have?

11. What was the name of the Mayan religious leader?

12. What sacrifice did many Mayan religious ceremonies include?

13. Why did the Mayan civilization end?

14. Whom did some Mayas meet in 1502?

Name ______________________________ Date ____________________

Fact or Opinion

To the left of each sentence write "F" if you believe the statement is a fact or an "O" if you believe it is an opinion.

_____ 1. The Mayas settled in the Yucatan Peninsula.

_____ 2. Tikal was the largest Mayan city.

_____ 3. Tikal was a better city than Copán.

_____ 4. The Mayas used glyphs instead of an alphabet.

_____ 5. Glyphs are better than an alphabet.

_____ 6. Ancient Mayas were more religious than modern Indians of Mayan descent.

_____ 7. European museums should return ancient Mayan books to Mexico.

_____ 8. The end of the Mayan civilization remains a mystery.

_____ 9. The Mayan civilization deserved to end.

_____ 10. Christopher Columbus met some Mayas.

Write an Eyewitness Account

Pretend you were a witness to Columbus meeting the Mayas. Describe what this meeting might have been like. Continue on your own paper, if necessary.

____

____

____

____

____

____

____

____

Name ______________________________ Date ________________

Making Comparisons

The column at the left gives statements about our modern culture. In the spaces at the right, give information from the article that tells of Mayan similarities or differences.

OUR CULTURE	THE MAYAN CULTURE
1. Our culture borrowed from the English culture.	1. ______________________________
2. The Statue of Liberty is one of our most famous structures.	2. ______________________________
3. We have advanced methods of agriculture.	3. ______________________________
4. We use an alphabet.	4. ______________________________
5. We manufacture paper and make books.	5. ______________________________
6. We use a zero.	6. ______________________________
7. Most of us believe in one supreme God or being.	7. ______________________________
8. We have a calendar with 365 days.	8. ______________________________
9. We have a calendar with 12 months.	9. ______________________________
10. We have a calendar with months (except February) of 30 or 31 days.	10. ______________________________

THE AZTECS

Tenochtitlan

The Aztec civilization was one of the most highly-developed Indian cultures of the Western Hemisphere. They had advanced methods of writing, mathematics, and agriculture. The Aztec religion and warfare helped advance their civilization throughout what is now Mexico.

The greatest city of the Aztecs was Tenochtitlan. It was on the site that is modern-day Mexico City. Tenochtitlan became the capital of the Aztec empire. Its population may have reached 200,000. There was a great plaza in the city's center, which measured 520 by 600 feet and contained over 60 buildings.

The Aztecs used a form of picture writing. Some pictures represented ideas, while other pictures represented sounds. Some modern words come from *Náhuatl,* the native Aztec language. Mexico, avocado, chocolate, and tomato are Aztec words.

The Aztec nation consisted of separate city-states. The largest city-states were Tenochtitlan, Texaco, and Tlatelolco.

The *calpolli,* or clan, was the basis of Aztec life. Each person was a member of a clan. Twenty clans formed a tribe. The calpolli owned the land and elected a council of members to govern. The council then chose a chief. A council chose the emperor from members of the royal family. The greatest Aztec emperor, Montezuma I, ruled from 1440 to 1468.

The Aztecs educated their children at home and in special clan schools. The family arranged for all marriages.

Agriculture was of major importance to the Aztecs. They cleared much land for farming. They also built *chinampas*. These were small islands created in shallow lakes and swamps. The Aztecs piled mud from the bottom of the lake or swamp into mounds or islands. They also cut terraces into hillsides to create more farmland. They made canals to carry water to their fields.

Aztec religion had over 60 gods and goddesses. Each village had a patron god. They also worshipped different gods for special purposes. They held many religious ceremonies and festivals. Many Aztec religious ceremonies included human sacrifice.

The Aztecs used two calendars. One was a lunar calendar, based on the phases of the Moon. Priests used this calendar to determine religious days and lucky days. The other was a solar calendar, based on the movement of the Sun. It is similar to the calendar we use today.

The Spanish government began sending expeditions into Mexico in 1517. The Spanish conquistador, Hernado Cortés, first invaded Mexico in search of gold in 1519. He and his soldiers conquered the Aztec empire in 1521. They destroyed the Aztec cities and made many of the Aztecs their slaves.

Aztec designs still have a strong influence on Mexican art and culture. Thousands of modern Mexicans are descendants of the Aztecs.

Name ____ Date ________________________

Questions for Consideration

1. What was the name of the greatest Aztec city?

2. What modern city is on the same site?

3. What form of writing did the Aztecs use?

4. What is a *calpolli?*

5. How many clans formed a tribe?

6. Who was the greatest Aztec emperor?

7. Who arranged Aztec marriages?

8. What is a *chinampas?*

9. How many gods and goddesses did the Aztecs worship?

10. What unusual thing did many Aztec religious ceremonies include?

11.–12. What two calendars did the Aztecs use?

13. When did Cortés first invade Mexico?

14. In what year did Cortés conquer the Aztec empire?

Name ______________________________ Date ____________________

Which Does Not Belong?

One word in each list below does not belong with the others. Circle the word in each group that is different. Tell why it is different on the line below each word group.

1. Mexico City	Tenochtitlan	Texaco	Tlatelolco

____

2. avocado	cabbage	chocolate	tomato

____

3. agriculture	mathematics	mass media	writing

____

4. Olmec	calpolli	chinampas	Náhuatl

____

5. made canals	made communes	made mounds	made terraces

____

Matching

Match the correct response in the second column with the corresponding item in the first column.

____	1. Tenochtitlan	A. A clan
____	2. Náhuatl	B. Islands
____	3. Calpolli	C. Human sacrifice
____	4. Montezuma	D. A calendar similar to our calendar today
____	5. Chinampas	E. The capital city
____	6. Religious ceremonies	F. Chose the emperor
____	7. Lunar	G. Conquered the Aztecs
____	8. Solar	H. A calendar used by Aztec priests
____	9. Cortés	I. The Aztec language
____	10. The council	J. A famous Aztec emperor

Name ______________________________ Date ____________________

Word Scramble

Unscramble the following groups of letters to form words that were used in the chapter on the Aztecs. Then give a brief description of each word.

1. ZEACT ______________________________

____

2. INNCTTTOHIEAL ______________________________

____

3. MOOTTA ______________________________

____

4. OLTECAOHC ______________________________

____

5. LALCLPIO ______________________________

____

6. ZOTAMMENU ______________________________

____

7. SHANCMAIP ______________________________

____

8. UMHNA CIFESIRAC ______________________________

____

9. AEDCNRSLA ______________________________

____

10. SRÉCTO ______________________________

____

THE SPANISH

The Spanish built many cathedrals in Mexico using architectural styles from their homeland.

The Spanish began settlements in the new world shortly after Columbus made his famous voyages. They first entered Mexico in 1517. Hernando Cortés and his soldiers defeated the Aztecs within just three years of their arrival in 1519. Cortés was looking for gold and other valuables, as well as slave labor.

Cortés named the territory *New Spain*. Spain appointed Cortés as the first governor of the new colony. The government gave special land grants to many of the early Spanish settlers.

During the next 250 years, over 300,000 Spaniards crossed the Atlantic Ocean to live in New Spain. They organized the new land into a unified Spanish-speaking territory. They established cities, industries, and large ranches. Throughout Spanish rule, leaders suppressed the Indian culture.

Four classes of people emerged in the colony. The *peninsulares* were those born in Spain who settled in the new land. The *criollos* were of full Spanish descent, but were born in the colony. The *mestizos* were of mixed Spanish and native Indian heritage. The Indians were of full native Indian descent. A class structure developed with the peninsulares at the top and the Indians at the bottom. The peninsulares made up less than one percent of the population, and yet they owned almost all of the land.

The Roman Catholic church began to send priests and missionaries into the new colony. Spanish religious groups, especially the Franciscans, began building monasteries and missions throughout Mexico and the southwestern United States. They built over 12,000 churches by 1800.

The Spanish colonists developed the land's resources. Cities emerged and the mining industry, large ranches, and farms also flourished. New Spain began to export vast amounts of wheat, sugarcane, cotton, and valuable ores to Spain. However, the Spanish refused to allow any industry or products from the new colony to compete with those already in Spain.

The economy of New Spain collapsed in the seventeenth century. Disease and overwork wiped out much of the Indian labor force. Overgrazing herds of animals destroyed much valuable farmland. A new Spanish royal family, the Bourbons, came to power in the eighteenth century. They reorganized the colony of New Spain, and the economy soon revived.

Feelings against Spanish control began to grow. Just as in the U.S. colonies, the citizens began to rebel against taxation and control by another nation. At the same time, the importance of Spain as a world power declined.

Several uprisings against Spanish control began. A priest named Miguel Hidalgo y Costilla led one of the more important revolts. The uprisings caused a great deal of bloodshed. The Spanish government always responded violently. They executed many revolutionary leaders. A final revolt led by Agustín de Iturbide won independence on September 27, 1821.

Name ______________________ Date ____________

Questions for Consideration

1. When did the Spanish first enter Mexico?

2. Who led the Spanish defeat of the Aztecs?

3. What was the name given the territory that is now Mexico?

4. How many Spaniards came to the new territory?

5. What are *peninsulares?*

6. What are *criollos?*

7. What are *mestizos?*

8. Which religious group of the Roman Catholic church was the major builder of missions in Mexico?

9. When did the economy of the territory collapse?

10. What was the name of the royal family that came to power in the eighteenth century?

11. What priest led an early revolt against Spanish rule?

12. When did Mexico get freedom from Spain?

Name ________________________________ Date ____________________

Arrange in Chronological Order

Indicate by number the order in which the following events occurred.

_____ 1. Over 12,000 churches are built in Mexico.

_____ 2. The Bourbon family comes to power in Spain.

_____ 3. Mexico gains independence.

_____ 4. The major migration of Spaniards to New Spain begins.

_____ 5. Christopher Columbus visits what is now Mexico.

_____ 6. Agustín de Iturbide begins his revolt.

_____ 7. The Spanish first enter Mexico.

_____ 8. Cortés is appointed governor of the territory.

_____ 9. The economy of New Spain collapses.

_____ 10. Cortés defeats the Aztecs.

Write a Biography

Many important and interesting individuals became part of the Spanish settlement of Mexico. Using other sources, research the story of one of the following people and write a brief story of his life.

Montezuma II (The last Aztec chief)

Hernado Cortés

Miguel Hidalgo y Costilla

Agustín de Iturbide

Name ______________________________ Date ____________________

Crossword Puzzle

Use the clues below to complete the puzzle. You can find the words in the narrative about the Spanish in Mexico.

ACROSS

2. The early Spanish explorers were looking for this.
3. The last name of the priest who led an early revolt against Spanish rule
4. European settlement of Mexico began after this man's famous voyages.
9. The name given to the territory that is now Mexico (two words).
11. Mexican citizens of full Spanish descent
13. The last name of the man who led the successful revolt that won Mexican independence
14. This and overwork wiped out much of the Indian labor force.

DOWN

1. This religious group sent priests to the new territory (two words).
3. Over 12,000 of these were built in Mexico by 1800.
5. The Spanish royal family that came to power in the eighteenth century
6. The month in which Mexico won its independence
7. People of mixed Spanish and Indian heritage
8. He defeated the Aztecs.
10. Three hundred thousand of these people came to the new territory.
12. The government gave ______ grants to many early settlers.

CORTÉS AND MONTEZUMA

At first, Montezuma welcomed Cortés and his men to the capital.

The Aztec civilization was at its peak when the Spanish began to settle in Mexico. The Spanish sent explorers into Mexico in 1517 and 1518. Hernado Cortés led the third expedition in 1519.

The Spaniards hoped to find gold and other valuable treasure. They also wanted to find slave labor for their sugar plantations in Cuba.

Cortés and his men first met the Aztecs in 1519. With help from other Indian tribes, the Spaniards conquered the Aztecs in only three years. These tribes were jealous of the Aztecs and resented paying taxes to the Aztec empire.

Montezuma II became emperor of the Aztecs in 1502. He was the grandson of the greatest Aztec emperor, Montezuma I. The people thought their emperor was a living god. He was an absolute ruler.

Montezuma did not fight against the Spaniards. He remembered a legend that said that the powerful god Quetzalcoatl sailed across the sea and would return someday. Cortés and his men were the first white men the Aztecs ever saw. Montezuma believed that Cortés was Quetzalcoatl. Montezuma thought Quetzalcoatl (Cortés) would come and reclaim the throne, so he sent valuable gifts to Cortés to buy him off and keep him out of the capital. However, the gifts only increased Cortés' interest in coming to the great city.

On November 8, 1519, Montezuma welcomed Cortés and his men into the capital city of Tenochtitlan. The Aztecs entertained Cortés and his men as if they were gods returning to their home lands.

The Spaniards could not believe what they saw. Tenochtitlan was a huge city, larger than any in Europe at the time. Its main plaza measured 520 by 600 feet. The great temple pyramid rose over 200 feet high. The emperor's palace, with its many richly decorated rooms and gardens, dazzled them. One of Cortés' men wrote that the city was like a dream.

Cortés and his men did not return the hospitality, however. They captured the city and made Montezuma their prisoner in his own city. When the Spaniards stopped one of the Aztec religious ceremonies, Montezuma tried to calm his people, but the Aztecs, angered by Montezuma, threw rocks at him.

The great Aztec emperor Montezuma died in 1521. His death happened at the same time as the last great battle that destroyed much of Tenochtitlan. No one knows if Cortés or the injuries suffered at the hands of his own people killed Montezuma. His death represented the end of the great Aztec nation.

The Spaniards continued to fight the Aztecs. They brought cannons, horses, and war dogs from Europe. The Indians had never seen these before. The Spanish then left the ruined city and continued their conquest of the rest of the Aztec empire.

Cortés continued to dominate the territory, but he returned to Spain to answer charges of corruption. He came back to Mexico and lived on a large ranch until 1547 when he returned to Spain. Cortés died in Seville, Spain, on December 2, 1547. The government returned his remains to Mexico for burial.

Name ______________________________ Date ____________________

Questions for Consideration

1. In what year did Cortés lead the third Spanish expedition into Mexico?

____

2. In what year did the Spaniards conquer the Aztecs?

____

3. When did Montezuma II become emperor of the Aztecs?

____

4. Whom did Montezuma believe Cortés was?

____

____

5. Why did Montezuma send gifts to Cortés?

____

____

6. When did Montezuma welcome Cortés into the capital city?

____

7. What did one of Cortés' men write about the city?

____

8. What did Cortés do to Montezuma?

____

____

9. What did the Aztecs do to Montezuma when he tried to calm them?

____

10. When did Montezuma die?

____

11. Where did Cortés die?

____

12. Where was Cortés buried?

____

Name ________________________________ Date ____________________

Write an Eyewitness Account

The meeting of the great Aztec emperor Montezuma and the Spanish military leader Cortés was one of the most unusual and interesting events in history. Pretend you are one of Cortés' men. Write an eyewitness account of this historic event.

Name ______________________________ Date ____________________

Using Divergent Thinking Skills

Divergent thinking involves taking an important event and imagining what it would have been like had it turned out in a different way. In the space below, write how you think history might have been different if Cortés had not defeated Montezuma.

An Art Activity

Make a poster of either Cortés or Montezuma in full costume.

Make a poster or shoebox diorama showing the meeting of Cortés and Montezuma.

INDEPENDENCE TO 1910

Miguel Hidalgo y Costilla

Conflict, crisis, and bloodshed fill Mexico's history. The Spaniards violently destroyed the Indian civilization. The Spanish colonial period lasted for about 300 years, but its government also ended in violence.

A poor priest, Miguel Hidalgo y Costilla, lead the first major revolt against Spanish control. The Spanish government crushed his rebellion and executed him in 1811.

A time of unhappiness and struggle followed. A second major rebellion, led by Augustin de Iturbide, finally won independence in 1821. Iturbide became a self-proclaimed emperor of Mexico. The following year, unpaid soldiers overthrew him. Guadalupe Victoria then became the first president of the new nation. However, Mexico remained in chaos for the next 50 years.

Historians refer to the years from 1823 to 1855 as the "Age of Santa Anna." General Antonio López de Santa Anna led the revolt to overthrow Iturbide. Santa Anna then served several terms as the president.

Two major political groups continued battling during this time. The liberals wanted to pattern the Mexican government after that of the United States. The conservatives wanted a more military-style government. The country continued to be in chaos, the economy fell apart, and the nation became bankrupt

During the Age of Santa Anna, Mexico went to war with Texas. Texas declared its independence from Mexico on March 2, 1836. Santa Anna won the famous battle at the Alamo on March 6, 1836. However, the Mexicans eventually lost the war. In 1846, disagreement over the boundary between Mexico and Texas, now a U.S. state, led to the beginning of the Mexican War. Land that is now part of Texas and most of northern Arizona, New Mexico, and California became the territory of the United States. Later, Santa Anna's government sold southern Arizona to the Untied States for $10 million.

The liberals forced Santa Anna from power and began to make several reforms. The conservatives asked for help from France.

The French, under Napoleon III set up a government headed by an Austrian archduke named Maximilian. Maximilian became the emperor of Mexico. He was a puppet of the French government. Maximilian was not able to unify the nation, and the French pulled their support out of the country in 1867. Maximilian lost his power and was court-martialed. He was executed by a firing squad on June 19, 1867.

For almost 10 years Mexico was in turmoil. General Porfirio Diaz seized power in 1876. He was the president from 1877 to 1880 and 1884 to 1910. Diaz made many reforms and helped improve the economic stability of the country. The civil wars ended. The economy improved, and several foreign investors brought money into the economy. Many building projects began.

In spite of the progress of the Diaz government, the majority of the population remained poor. They resented Diaz's monopoly of political power. They also hated the foreign control of industry. Revolts against the Diaz government began. Strikes against a copper company and a textile mill began a new revolution. The revolution of 1910 brought about the end of the Diaz era.

Name ______________________________ Date ____________________

Questions for Consideration

1. What did the priest Miguel Hidalgo y Costilla do that made him important in Mexican history?

____

2. Who led the final rebellion that won independence?

____

3. Who became the first president of Mexico?

____

4. Who ruled Mexico from 1823 to 1855?

____

5. What famous battle did this ruler win?

____

6. What war did this ruler lose?

____

7. Who was the emperor of Mexico set up by the French government?

____

8. What finally happened to this emperor?

____

9. Who was the major leader of Mexico from 1876 until 1910?

____

10.–11. What were two major reasons the masses rebelled against this leader?

____

____

____

12.–13. In what industries did strikes begin the revolution of 1910?

____

____

Name ______________________________ Date ____________________

Increasing Your Vocabulary

The following is a list of words used in the narration about Mexico's struggle for independence that you may not fully understand. Look them up in a dictionary and write their meanings. Also, write a sentence using each word correctly.

1. colonial ______________________________

____

2. rebellion ______________________________

____

3. proclaimed ______________________________

____

4. chaos ______________________________

____

5. conservative ______________________________

____

6. liberal ______________________________

____

7. court-martial ______________________________

____

8. turmoil ______________________________

____

9. stability ______________________________

____

10. monopoly ______________________________

____

Name ______________________________ Date ____________________

Sequencing

Indicate by number the order in which the following events occurred in Mexico's struggle for independence.

_____ 1. Maximilian becomes emperor

_____ 2. Iturbide becomes emperor

_____ 3. Victoria becomes president

_____ 4. Diaz becomes president

_____ 5. Santa Anna becomes president

_____ 6. Mexico sells southern Arizona to the United States

_____ 7. The Spanish colonial period grows

_____ 8. Texas declares independence

_____ 9. Costilla leads revolt

_____ 10. Battle of the Alamo

Fact or Opinion

To the left of each sentence, write "F" if you think the statement is a fact and "O" if you think it is an opinion.

_____ 1. The Spanish crushed Costilla's rebellion.

_____ 2. Costilla was a bad leader.

_____ 3. Costilla should not have tried to rebel against the Spanish.

_____ 4. Santa Anna was a better president than Diaz.

_____ 5. Diaz was president longer than Santa Anna.

_____ 6. Maximilian was supported by France and the conservatives.

_____ 7. The liberals should have supported Maximilian.

_____ 8. Diaz improved the Mexican economy.

_____ 9. Diaz had a monopoly of political power.

_____ 10. Diaz deserved to be overthrown by the revolution.

SANTA ANNA

(1795?–1876)

Santa Anna

Antonio López de Santa Anna was a Mexican general, revolutionary, and president. He was born at Jalapa on February 21, 1795(?). His father was a government official. Santa Anna joined the army at the age of 15. He supported Augustin de Iturbide's revolt against Spanish control, but later, Santa Anna led a rebellion against Iturbide.

Mexico experienced great unrest during the next several years, and Santa Anna continued his involvement in government affairs. Santa Anna served as minister of war and commander-in-chief of the federal forces. He became president for the first time in 1833. He was popular with the military, but not with many of the people. After defeating an opposition army, he became dictator. He then strengthened the central power of the government and abolished the constitution.

Texas declared its independence from Mexico, and Santa Anna attacked San Antonio in 1836. His army defeated the Texans at the battle of the Alamo. Later, Santa Anna lost the Battle of San Jacinto on April 21, 1836. The Texans captured and took him prisoner. In exchange for his release, he agreed to grant Texas its independence.

Santa Anna retired after returning to Mexico in 1837. Within a year, though, he came out of retirement and led the army to victory in an assault on Veracruz. He lost a leg during the battle, but his victory made him a hero to the Mexican people. He became the president again from 1841 to 1844.

In 1845, enemies overthrew him. They took him prisoner and banished him. Soon, however, the government recalled him to lead Mexico against the United States in the Mexican War.

In 1847, Santa Anna led Mexican forces against the American troops of General Zachary Taylor. Taylor defeated Santa Anna at the famous battle of Buena Vista. This victory later helped Taylor become president of the United States. The Americans, under the leadership of General Winfield Scott, again defeated Santa Anna at the battle of Cerro Gordo. The Americans soon won the war and entered Mexico City. Santa Anna resigned, and he received permission to leave the country. He then lived in Jamaica and Venezuela.

The government again brought Santa Anna back to power in 1853. This time he declared that he was president for life. However, another revolution defeated him just one year later. He fled from Mexico and lived in Cuba, Venezuela, and Saint Thomas. While he was in exile, the new government found him guilty of treason.

Santa Anna returned to Mexico when the French controlled the government, but was not allowed to stay. He then spent some time in exile in the United States. The government granted him amnesty in 1874 and allowed him to return to Mexico.

Santa Anna died in Mexico City on June 20, 1876.

Name ______________________ Date ______________

Questions for Consideration

1. What was Santa Anna's father's occupation?

____

2. Whom did Santa Anna first support and then lead a rebellion against?

____

3. When did Santa Anna become Mexico's president for the first time?

____

4. What city did Santa Anna attack in 1836?

____

5. In what famous battle did Santa Anna defeat the Texans?

____

6. What did Santa Anna grant in exchange for being released as a prisoner?

____

____

7. What did Santa Anna lose during the battle of Veracruz?

____

8. What future U.S. president did Santa Anna fight against in the Mexican War?

____

9.–10. What were the two most famous battles of the Mexican War that the Americans won?

____

____

11. Of what did the government of Mexico find Santa Anna guilty?

____

12. When did Santa Anna die?

____

Name ______________________________ Date ____________________

Map Activity

Using an atlas to help, label the following locations that were important in the life of Santa Anna.

Cities:

SAN ANTONIO, TEXAS MEXICO CITY, MEXICO

Countries:

CUBA JAMAICA SAINT THOMAS VENEZUELA

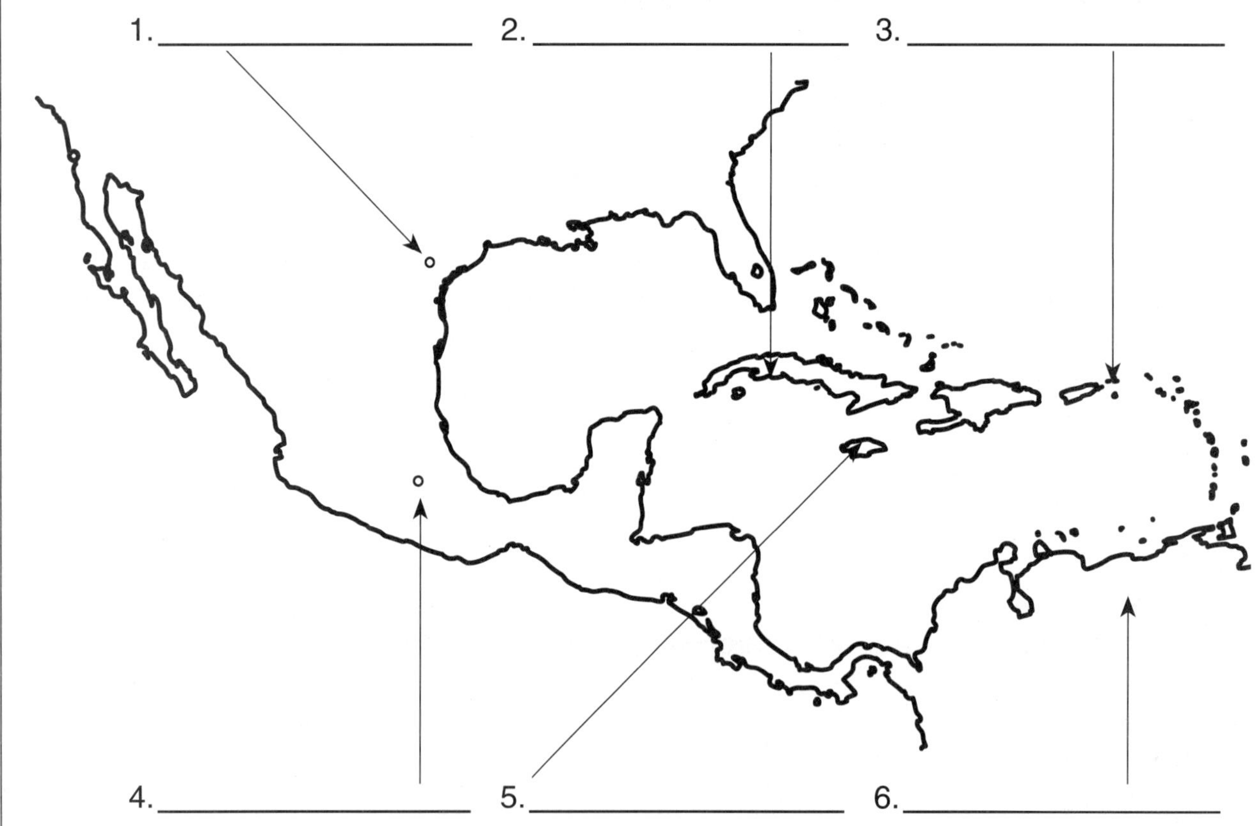

Name ______________________________ Date ____________________

For Further Research

On your own paper, write a one-page report on one of the following topics:

Zachary Taylor   The Mexican War   The Battle of the Alamo

Be Part of a Press Conference

Santa Anna led an amazing life. Pretend you are a reporter at a press conference held for Santa Anna in 1874, when he returned to Mexico for the last time. Write out three questions that you might have asked him. Then write out what you believe he might have said in response to each question.

First Question: ____

____

Response: ____

____

____

____

Second Question: ____

____

Response: ____

____

____

____

Third Question: ____

____

Response: ____

____

____

____

AFTER REVOLUTION

Emiliano Zapata

The revolution of 1910 toppled the government of Porfirio Diaz. His government collapsed, and Diaz fled. During the next few years, several leaders seized power, only to be overthrown themselves. Many of the changes of government happened with much violence.

Francisco I. Madero led the revolt against Diaz. Madero won the presidency in late 1911, but his government only lasted 15 months. During this time, his government had to fight six major rebellions.

Victoriano Huerta overthrew Madero. He dissolved the congress and then arrested its members. His army soon executed Madero and hundreds of others. Huerta's new government soon faced several rebellions against its power.

In the north, a former bandit named Francisco (known as Pancho) Villa, organized a band of local cowboys. Villa and his men made many raids throughout Mexico and into the United States. Villa remains one of the great folk heroes of Mexican history.

In the south, a farmer named Emiliano Zapata organized the landless peasants. He fought under the slogan "land and liberty and death to the hacendados (landowners)." He and his men seized ranches, drove the owners out, and then divided the land among the peasants. For a while Zapata and Villa joined together against common enemies.

Many other groups fought against the Huerta government. The United States, under President Woodrow Wilson, stepped in and helped oust Huerta.

In 1914, Venustiano Carranza assumed power. His party drafted the constitution of 1917. His government became involved in a civil war with the forces of both Villa and Zapata. Carranza's army eventually won. Zapata was murdered in 1919, and Villa surrendered in 1920. Political enemies shot Villa in 1923.

In 1920, General Alvaro Obregón overthrew Carranza's government. Enemies killed Carranza as he fled Mexico City.

Several governments ruled from 1921 to 1933. They became known as the "Northern Dynasty" since all of the presidents came from northern Mexico. Northern Dynasty presidents included Alvaro Obregón and Plutarco Calles. Their governments established some order and worked to develop the economy. They faced opposition from the clergy, landowners, and foreign investors. While in power, the Northern Dynasty government crushed several rebellions.

In 1934, the election of General Lázaro Cárdenas ended the era of the Northern Dynasty. He made land reforms, organized labor, and increased national control of many industries. He forced out foreign oil companies and placed the oil industry under Mexican government control.

Cárdenas left office peacefully in 1940. His administration did much to solidify Mexican politics and prepare his country for the modern world.

Name ____________________ Date ____________

Questions for Consideration

1. Who led the revolt against the Diaz government?

___

2. How long did his government last?

___

3.–4. What two things did Victoriano Huerta do to the Mexican congress?

___

___

___

5. What former bandit is a Mexican folk hero?

___

6. What farmer organized the famous peasant revolt?

___

7. What U.S. president sent troops to help oust Huerta?

___

8. What Mexican president had his party draft the constitution of 1917?

___

9. What name is used to label the governments of Mexico from 1921 to 1933?

___

10. Who became Mexico's president in 1934?

___

11. What did he do to the oil industry?

___

___

___

Name ______________________________ Date ________________

Mexico's Presidents

Below is a list of the presidents of Mexico since the revolution of 1910. In addition, there were eight men who were interim (served between the regular) presidents. Use this list to answer the questions in the right column.

Francisco I. Madero	1911–1913
Venustiano Carranza	1914 and 1915–1920
Roque Gonzalez Garza	1914
Francisco Lagos Cházaro	1915
Alvaro Obregón	1920–1924
Plutarco Elías Calles	1924–1928
Pascual Ortiz Rubio	1930–1932
Lázaro Cárdenas	1934–1940
Manuel Avila Camacho	1940–1946
Miguel Alemán Valdés	1946–1952
Adolfo Ruiz Cortines	1952–1958
Adolfo López Mateos	1958–1964
Gustavo Díaz Ordaz	1964–1970
Luis Echeverría Alvarez	1970–1976
José López Portillo	1976–1982
Miguel de la Madrid	1982–1988
Carlos Salinas de Gortari	1988–1994
Ernesto Zedillo	1994–

1. During the 1920s, how long was the term of office of a Mexican president?

____

2. After the 1930s, how long was the term of office of a Mexican president?

____

3. Which president had a divided term of office?

____

4. Which president served during World War II?

____

5. Which was the last president mentioned in the narrative?

____

Name ______________________________ Date ____________________

What Do You Think?

Mexico's history is filled with violence and unrest. Mexico had 16 presidents and interim presidents from 1910 until 1940. During this same time, the United States had six. Write a short response to the two questions below.

1. Why do you think Mexico had so many presidents compared to the United States during this time?

____

____

____

____

____

____

____

____

____

2. How would having so many presidents hurt a country?

____

____

____

____

____

____

____

____

____

____

FRANCISCO "PANCHO" VILLA

(1878–1923)

Pancho Villa

Pancho Villa remains one of Mexico's most interesting folk heroes. Many consider him to be Mexico's Robin Hood, since he took from the rich and helped the poor of his country.

Villa was born in Hacienda de Río Grande, Durango, on June 5,1878. His parents named him Doroteo Arango. As a youth, he killed a man to protect his sister. He then borrowed the name "Francisco Villa." It was the name of a noted outlaw of the time.

Villa became a bandit early in his life. In 1903, Mexican troops captured him. They allowed him to avoid prison, however, if he agreed to join a military regiment, but Villa soon returned to crime. He robbed trains and banks and raided mines.

He joined Francisco Madero's uprising against the dictator Porfirio Diaz in 1909. The outbreak of the revolution occurred in 1910. Villa won fame as a fighter in the 1911 battle at Juárez. He captured Juárez in 1911 and again in 1913 and 1919. He also repeatedly captured other cities.

Villa argued with fellow revolutionary Victoriano Huerta. When Huerta gained power in 1912, he imprisoned Villa, but Villa escaped just four months later and moved to El Paso, Texas. He reorganized his followers and returned to Mexico in 1913. Villa named his followers the "Division del Norte" (the Division of the North). During the next two years, Villa defeated many competitors for the Mexican presidency. U.S. President Woodrow Wilson sent a representative, George C. Cruthers, to aid Villa.

Villa then joined with Venustiano Carranza. They fought against Victoriano Huerta in 1914. The two men then became rivals, and Villa fled to the mountains.

Villa lost the Battle of Celaya to General Alvaro Obregón in 1915. Many of Villa's supporters joined Obregón and Carranza after Villa's defeat.

The United States then shifted its support from Villa to Carranza. Villa and his men felt betrayed. For revenge, they killed 15 Americans in the Santa Isabel Massacre in January, 1916. Villa's troops then raided Columbus, New Mexico, on March 9, 1916, killing 17 Americans. The United States sent General John J. Pershing to punish Villa. Pershing's men killed several of Villa's followers, but they did not capture Villa. He and only three of his men escaped.

The Mexican government pardoned Villa in 1920. He retired as a general with full pay, and, in exchange for a ranch, he agreed to retire from politics.

Villa was not to be left in peace, however. His enemies used a pumpkin-seed vender to alert them as Villa approached, and they killed him in his automobile. Villa died on July 20, 1923, near Parral, Mexico.

In 1927, someone opened his tomb and stole his skull. Police never discovered who did this. The skull is still missing.

Villa is still popular with the masses. Even though he killed many people, he is considered a folk hero because he fought for the rights of the common man. Mexicans remember Villa for helping the poor and suffering of his nation.

Name ______________________________ Date ____________________

Questions for Consideration

1. To what other folk hero is Villa often compared?

____

2. From whom did he borrow the name Francisco Villa?

____

3. What Mexican leader did Villa join to fight against Diaz?

____

4. In what battle did Villa first win fame?

____

5. In what American city did Villa live for a while?

____

6. What did Villa name his followers?

____

7. What U.S. president sent someone to aid Villa?

____

8. What important battle did Villa lose in 1915?

____

9. What did Villa do in revenge for the United States change of support from him?

____

____

10. What U.S. general pursued Villa?

____

11. What did the Mexican government do to Villa in 1920?

____

____

12. How did Villa die?

____

____

Name ______________________________ Date ____________________

Arrange in Chronological Order

By using letters of the alphabet, indicate the order in which the following events occurred in the life of Pancho Villa.

_____ 1. Captures Juárez the first time

_____ 2. Organizes Division del Norte

_____ 3. Agrees to join military regiment to avoid prison

_____ 4. Loses battle of Celaya

_____ 5. Mexican government pardons him

_____ 6. He borrows the name "Francisco Villa"

_____ 7. President Woodrow Wilson aids him

_____ 8. Moves to El Paso

_____ 9. General John J. Pershing pursues him

_____ 10. Joins Madero against Díaz

Write a Letter

Pancho Villa was a thief and a murderer. He also was kind to the poor and often helped them. Write a letter to Villa, in which you tell him what you think of his activities.

Dear Mr. Villa,

____

____

____

____

____

____

____

Sincerely,

____

Name ______________________________ Date ____________________

Make a Poster

Pancho Villa is a Mexican folk hero. However, at one time he was wanted by the government of the United States for the murder of 32 Americans. Below, make a wanted poster for Villa. Find a picture in a book or encyclopedia as a guide to illustrate the poster. Write out the details of his crime and the reward offered.

MODERN MEXICO

Oil refineries are a major part of Mexico's economy.

During World War II, Mexico joined the Allies. It supplied many raw materials for the war effort to the United States.

Mexico's population exploded after the war, and it continues to grow 50 percent faster than the world average. The rapid population growth continues to increase Mexico's unemployment rate.

After World War II, the military became less involved in politics, and politics became less violent. Peaceful changes in administrations have continued since 1946. Women received the vote in 1958.

Economic and industrial growth continues. Mexico increases its industrial production annually. Many major foreign companies have invested in factories recently. Oil is now Mexico's major industry. Explorers discovered new major oil reserves in 1976. These reserves may be the largest oil find in the Western Hemisphere.

Mexico took out many huge international loans to help build its economy. The country borrowed over $80 billion. It planned to pay back the loans with profits from oil sales. However, the decline of oil prices in the 1980s plunged Mexico into an economic crisis. It was not able to pay back the loans. By 1989, Mexico had a foreign debt of over $100 billion and a national debt of over $50 billion. The national debt and an unfavorable balance of trade continue to plague the government.

The great earthquake of 1985 added to Mexico's problems. The quake killed thousands of people and destroyed hundreds of buildings. It also interrupted several programs to improve the economy. In 1988, hurricane Gilbert damaged major resorts in Cancún and Cozumel.

The uneven distribution of wealth continues. A very small percentage of the people have a great deal of the wealth, while the majority of Mexico's people live in poverty.

Some rebellion against Mexico's problems has arisen. The government brutally ended a student protest in 1968. The election of 1988 almost brought another revolution. In 1993, more than 145 people died in riots demanding better working conditions, food, housing, and social programs

Relations between Mexico and the United States became strained in the 1990s. The United States blamed Mexico for not working to stop the flow of drugs and illegal immigrants across the border.

Mexico may be at a turning point in its history. It signed the North American Free Trade Agreement with Canada and the United States in 1992, and its economy is beginning to show signs of recovery.

Name _______________ Date _______________

Questions for Consideration

1. How did Mexico help the United States during World War II?

2. How does Mexico's population growth compare to the world average?

3. What other problem does Mexico's population growth make worse?

4. When did women receive the right to vote in Mexico?

5. What is Mexico's major industry?

6. Why was Mexico unable to repay its international loans?

7. What was Mexico's foreign debt by 1989?

8. What disaster hurt Mexico in 1985?

9. What disaster hurt Mexico in 1988?

10.–11. What two things does the United States want Mexico to help stop coming across the border?

12. What major agreement did Mexico, Canada, and the United States sign in 1992?

Name ______________________ Date ______________

Using a Bar Graph

Below is a bar graph showing Mexico's population growth. Using the graph, answer the following questions.

______________ 1. What was the population of Mexico in 1950?

______________ 2. In what year did Mexico's population reach 50 million people?

______________ 3. What happened to the population from 1960 to 1980?

______________ 4. Which decade (10 years) had the smallest population growth?

______________ 5. Which decade (10 years) had the largest population growth?

Mexico's Population 1940–1990

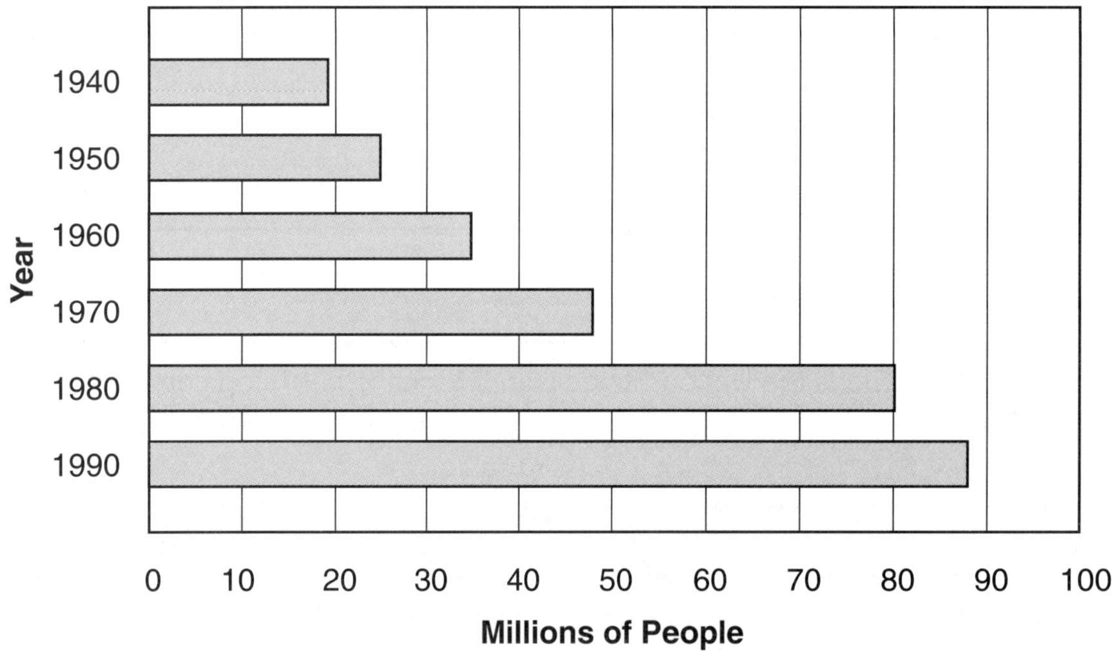

Name ________________________________ Date ____________________

Join a Press Conference

Pretend you are a reporter who will attend a joint press conference with the presidents of Mexico and the United States. In the spaces below, think of seven questions that you would like to ask Mexico's president and three questions about Mexican-American relationships you would like to ask the U.S. president.

QUESTIONS FOR MEXICO'S PRESIDENT:

Question 1: ____

____

Question 2: ____

____

Question 3: ____

____

Question 4: ____

____

Question 5: ____

____

Question 6: ____

____

Question 7: ____

____

QUESTIONS FOR THE U.S. PRESIDENT:

Question 1: ____

____

Question 2: ____

____

Question 3: ____

____

MEXICO CITY

Mexico City contains a mixture of modern, Spanish colonial, and Indian architecture.

Mexico City (*Ciudad de México* in Spanish) is the capital of Mexico. It is also one of the world's largest cities. The city's population is over 10 million, and the population of the metropolitan area is about 18 million.

Like the country of Mexico, Mexico City has many contrasts. Skyscrapers tower over Indian ruins and Spanish colonial buildings. People of great wealth live just a short distance from large slums. It is both an ancient and a modern city.

Mexico City lies on the ruins of the Aztec capital Tenochtitlan. It is in the southern part of the Mexican plateau and is surrounded by mountains. It has a high elevation of 7,556 feet above sea level. Because of its elevation, the climate is cool.

Mexico City is the country's leading industrial center. Its businesses produce over half of the nation's total output. Over 60 percent of the manufacturing jobs are in the city.

Pollution is a major problem in the city. The government shut down one major oil refinery and now refuses to let new polluting industries move into the area. Pollution from millions of motor vehicles also adds to the problem. Visitors often complain of a grayish-yellow smog that burns their eyes and throats.

Increasing population growth is another major problem for the city. The population quadrupled from 1950 to 1990. This means it doubled about every 10 years. The crime rates have increased along with the expanding population.

Earthquakes are common in Mexico City. The city is built on the bed of a former lake. Because of this, the soil is not as solid as in most places. When an earthquake strikes, the soil gives more. This causes earthquakes in the region to be even more destructive. On September 19 and 21, 1985, major earthquakes struck the city. They destroyed hundreds of buildings and killed over 20,000 people.

In spite of its problems, Mexico City is a popular tourist attraction. It is a major shopping center, including exclusive shops and department stores, as well as open-air markets. The city has many interesting and historic buildings and tree-lined boulevards, as well as large parks and plazas.

Important sites in the city include the National Cathedral, begun in 1573. It is the oldest and largest cathedral in the Western Hemisphere. Tourists can also visit the ruins of the major Aztec plaza and temple discovered in 1978. The city also contains the largest market in North America, Maximilian's castle, and the huge Plaza México.

Mexico City is also the nation's cultural center. It has many educational institutions including the National University. The National Museum of History, the Museum of Anthropology, and other museums and art galleries attract millions of visitors each year.

Name ______________________________ Date ______________

Questions for Consideration

1. What is Mexico City in Spanish?

____

2. What is the population of the city?

____

3. What is the population of the metropolitan area?

____

4. Mexico City is on the same location as what ancient city?

____

5. Why does Mexico City have a cool climate?

____

____

6. How many of Mexico's manufacturing jobs are in Mexico City?

____

7. Why did the government shut down an oil refinery in Mexico City?

____

____

8. What disaster happened in Mexico City in 1985?

____

____

9.–12. Name four of the tourist sites in Mexico City mentioned in the narrative.

____

____

____

____

13. What major educational institution is in Mexico City?

____

Name ______________________________ Date ______________

Good and Bad

Mexico City, like any major city, has both its good and its bad points. In the blanks below, list five good things and five bad things about Mexico's capital city.

GOOD

1. ______________________________
2. ______________________________
3. ______________________________
4. ______________________________
5. ______________________________

BAD

1. ______________________________
2. ______________________________
3. ______________________________
4. ______________________________
5. ______________________________

Art Activity

Make a poster or set of posters for Mexico City's tourist office. What would make tourists interested in visiting Mexico's capital? Find a book on Mexico City or look it up in an encyclopedia to find pictures to give you ideas.

Name ______________________ Date ______________

Crossword Puzzle

Use the clues below to complete the puzzle. You can find the words in the narrative about Mexico City.

ACROSS

1. One of Mexico City's problems, which caused the government to close an oil refinery.
3. ______ *de México* is "Mexico City" in Spanish.
5. Mexico City's population did this from 1950 to 1990.
9. This disaster hit Mexico City in 1985.
11. One of the major tourist attractions is Maximilian's ______.
12. Mexico City is located on this plateau.
13. Buildings of this colonial style are still in Mexico City.

DOWN

1. Mexico City's _____ is over 10 million.
2. Mexico City is the _____ of Mexico.
3. This Mexico City structure is the largest building of its kind in the Western Hemisphere.
4. Mexico City contains the largest one of these in North America.
6. Mexico City is on the site of an ancient city of this Indian civilization.
7. Mexico City is the location of the National Museum of ______.
8. Mexico City's elevation is 7,556 feet above this (two words).
10. Mexico's largest educational institution is the National______.

THE CITIES OF MEXICO

Mexico has many beachfront resort cities.

Mexico has many interesting and important cities in addition to Mexico City. This narrative briefly discusses just a few of them.

Several Mexican **towns on the border with the United States** are popular with tourists. Each year, millions of Americans cross the border to visit these towns. They give some idea of Mexican culture, but are geared toward visitors more than cities farther into Mexico. Tijuana, Mexicali, Juárez, and Nogales are the most noted border towns.

Acapulco is on the Pacific Ocean coast in southwest Mexico. It was once a major shipping town. Now Acapulco is a major vacation area. Modern hotels and resorts line its sandy beaches.

Cancún was a small fishing village in 1970. Today it is one of Mexico's major resort areas. It has grown so recently that it is not in many older atlases. It is second only to Acapulco as a resort area. Many modern hotels now line its white sand beaches. The ruins of the famous ancient Mayan city of Chichén Itzá are just a few miles away.

Cozumel is an island. The city's official name is San Miguel, but most refer to the city as Cozumel. It is another of Mexico's famous resorts.

Guadalajara is Mexico's second-largest city. It has a mild climate and a more relaxed pace than Monterrey or Mexico City. It is the capital of the state of Jalisco. It is in the center of a major agricultural region. It has many buildings in the Spanish style.

Mazatlán is one of Mexico's resort towns. It is on the western coast, just a few miles south of the Tropic of Cancer. It has a tropical climate. The coastline is full of modern hotels, but the old city keeps much of its Mexican atmosphere.

Monterrey is Mexico's third-largest city. It is mainly an industrial city. Mountains surround the city. The center of the city is the Plaza Zaragoza. Surrounding the plaza are the cathedral, government buildings, and shops.

Puerto Vallarta is another of Mexico's famous resort towns. It is located near the middle of Mexico's Pacific coast. It is quieter and less developed than Acapulco.

Teotihuacán is the site of ruins of an ancient city that reached its peak around A.D. 600. It is about 50 miles northeast of Mexico City. Ruins remain of the famous Pyramids of the Sun and Moon, the Temple of Quetzalcoatl, and the Temple of the Jaguars. Teotihuacán is a popular tourist destination.

Veracruz is rich in history. It was the first town founded in Mexico by the Spanish. It was the site of many invasions and military battles. A favorite tourist site is the Castillo de San Juan de Ulúa, which is a large fortress built by the Spanish to protect the port.

Name ______________________________ Date ____________________

Questions for Consideration

1.– 4. What cities mentioned in the narrative are on the U.S.-Mexican border?

____

____

5. What city mentioned is near the Tropic of Cancer?

____

6. What is Mexico's third-largest city?

____

7. What is Mexico's second-largest city?

____

8. What city contains the Pyramids of the Moon and Sun?

____

9. What resort town is a former shipping center?

____

10. What city is one of Mexico's newest resort areas?

____

11. Which of Mexico's resort towns is near the middle of its Pacific coast?

____

12. What city was the first founded by the Spanish?

____

13. Which city is on an island?

____

14. What city is near the ruins of Chichén Itzá?

____

Name ____________________ Date ____________

Map Exercise

Using an atlas to help, locate the following cities of Mexico:

ACAPULCO	CANCÚN	COZUMEL	GUADALAJARA
JUÁREZ	MAZATLÁN	MEXICO CITY	MONTERREY
PUERTO VALLARTA		TIJUANA	VERACRUZ

Name ______________________________ Date ____________________

Planning a Trip

Tourism is a major industry in Mexico. Visitors come for a variety of reasons. If you were planning a trip to Mexico, list the cities you would visit for the following reasons.

Resorts and sunny beaches:

1. ______________________________
2. ______________________________
3. ______________________________
4. ______________________________
5. ______________________________

A short visit just across the border:

6. ______________________________
7. ______________________________
8. ______________________________
9. ______________________________

Ancient Indian sites:

10. ______________________________
11. ______________________________

Mexico's industries (in addition to Mexico City):

12. ______________________________

Mexico's Spanish heritage

13. ______________________________
14. ______________________________

MEXICO'S GOVERNMENT

The Mexican National Palace

Mexico, like the United States, is a Federal Republic. The Constitution of 1917 established the current form of government. The government requires all persons over the age of 18 to vote.

Mexico has 31 states and a federal district. Mexico City is the federal district for the country.

Each state has a governor and a legislature. Each governor serves a six-year term and may not serve more than one term. Each state has a unicameral (one-house) legislature named the Chamber of Deputies. Each state's Chamber has from nine to 25 members. A deputy may serve only one consecutive term.

Mexico also has over 2,400 cities or townships called municipalities. Each municipality has its own government.

The federal government has three branches: the executive, the legislative, and the judicial branch.

The president is the head of the executive branch. The president serves a six-year term, and he or she may serve only one term. Mexico does not have a vice president. If the president is unable to finish the term, the Congress chooses a temporary president. The Mexican president has more power than the U.S. President. In addition to making major appointments and signing legislation, the current president names his successor to run for the office of president from his political party.

The legislative branch, the Congress, has a Senate and a Chamber of Deputies. The Senate has 64 members. Two members represent each state and two members represent the federal district. Each Senate member serves a six-year term. The Chamber of Deputies has 500 members. Each deputy serves a three-year term. Members of Congress cannot serve two terms in a row. The people directly elect three-fourths of the deputies. One-fourth of the deputies are selected in proportion to the votes received by each political party.

The judicial branch includes the Supreme Court of Justice, the highest court. Each state has a superior court. In addition, 21 circuit and 68 district courts serve the nation. Judges' appointments are for life.

Mexico's major political party is the *Partido Revolucionario Institutional* (the Institutional Revolutionary Party). The party, created in 1929, is known as the PRI. For many years, it was the only political party with any power. It suffered its first major defeat in 1997. It lost control of the Chamber of Deputies that year.

In recent years a second party the PAN, or *Partio de Acción Nacional* (National Action Party), has grown. Mexico also has several smaller political parties.

Name ______________________ Date ______________

Questions for Consideration

1. What established Mexico's current government?

____

____

2. How many states does Mexico have?

____

3. What is a unicameral legislature?

____

____

4. How many municipalities does Mexico have?

____

5.–7. What are the three branches of Mexico's government?

____

____

8. How long is the term of office of Mexico's president?

____

9.–10. What are the two houses of Mexico's legislature?

____

____

11. What is the highest court of Mexico?

____

12. What is Mexico's major political party (in English)?

____

Name ______________________________ Date ____________________

Making Comparisons

The government of Mexico is similar to that of the United States. However, the two governments also have many differences. In the spaces at the right, give information from the article that explains the similarities or differences.

UNITED STATES GOVERNMENT	MEXICO'S GOVERNMENT
1. Is a federal republic	1. ____________________
2. Has 50 states	2. ____________________
3. Each state (except one) has a two-house legislature	3. ____________________
4. Has three branches: executive, legislative, and judicial	4. ____________________
5. President's term is four years	5. ____________________
6. President may serve two terms	6. ____________________
7. Has a vice president	7. ____________________
8. Senate has 100 members	8. ____________________
9. House of Representatives has 435 members	9. ____________________
10. Members of Congress may serve several terms in a row	10. ____________________

Name ________________________________ Date ____________________

Building Your Political Vocabulary

You are familiar with many of the terms used in the narrative about Mexico's government. Others may be new to you. Using a dictionary, write out the exact meaning of the following terms.

1. Federal: ____

2. Republic: ____

3. Executive: ____

4. Legislative: ____

5. Judicial: ____

6. Successor: ____

7. Consecutive: ____

THE FIESTA

A fiesta is a celebration. Most fiestas are observances of religious holidays. Other festivals mark national historic holidays. Mexico has more fiestas than any other Latin American country. Most villages have local fiestas in addition to the national celebrations.

Many fiestas are lively, colorful celebrations, but some of the celebrations are more serious ceremonies. Most fiestas last one or two days. However, some fiestas can last up to a week.

The fiesta usually happens around the church or main plaza. A fiesta often includes open-air markets, folk dances, colorful costumes, decorations, flowers, parades, and fireworks. Music and dancing are always an important part of any fiesta. Fiestas also include a variety of special food and drink.

The *piñata* is often the children's most popular part of a fiesta. It is a colorful container filled with candy, toys, and money. Blindfolded children take turns swinging at a piñata suspended by a rope. When the piñata breaks, the children scramble to gather the presents. Originally piñatas were made from clay pots. Today, most piñatas are paper-mâché

The Feast of Our Lady of Guadalupe on December 12 is an important celebration. The main fiesta is in Mexico City. However, Mexicans celebrate the holiday throughout the nation. The fiesta celebrates the day the Virgin Mary made an appearance to an Indian peasant. Many make a pilgrimage to her church, the Basilica of the Virgin. Celebrations begin with traditional songs and dances the evening before. Many Christmas activities begin at this celebration.

Feliz Navidad is Spanish for Merry Christmas. Mexicans celebrate in many of the same ways as in the rest of the world. Celebrations include presents, holiday decorations, special foods, Christmas songs, and religious ceremonies. *Las Posada* is the main Christmas celebration. Spanish missionaries brought the celebration to Mexico. The poinsettia, the traditional Christmas flower, originally came from Mexico.

The most important festival of the year is a somber celebration. It is the Day of the Dead, in which the spirits of the dead are honored. The Spanish introduced the ceremony into Mexico. The celebration also blends in ancient Aztec beliefs. October 31 is *muertitos chicos,* the day for the souls of dead children to return. They believe adult souls return the following night. The main flower used for decoration is the marigold, because the Aztecs believed the marigold was sacred to the dead.

People leave a feast out for the dead. They bake special breads in human forms and in the shape of skulls. They believe the dead eat the spirit of the food. The living then eat the food the following day in remembrance of the dead.

Often, people keep an all-night candlelight vigil in the town cemetery, and families gather at the graves of relatives.

Major Mexican Holidays

(Individual communities have their own celebrations, often to commemorate their patron saints.)

January	1	New Year's Day
February	5	Constitution Day
March	21	Birthday of Benito Juárez
	Varies	Holy Week - The week prior to Easter
	Varies	Easter
May	1	Labor Day
June	24	Day of St. John, Midsummer's day
July	25	Day of St. James
August	15	Day of the Virgin de la Asunción
	25	Day of San Luis
September	16	Independence Day
October	12	Dia de la Raza - Day of the Races, celebrates the mix of cultures and races that became Mexico
November	1–2	Day of the Dead - All Saints' Day - All Souls' Day
	20	Anniversary of Mexican Revolution
	22	Day of St. Cecilia
December	12	Feast of Our Lady of Guadalupe
	17–24	Las Posada
	25	Christmas

Name ______________________________ Date ______________

Questions for Consideration

1. What is a fiesta?

____

____

2. Which Latin American country has the most fiestas?

____

3. How long do most fiestas last?

____

4. Where do most fiestas happen?

____

5. What is a *piñata?*

____

____

6. Where is the main celebration of the Feast of Our Lady of Guadalupe held?

____

7. When is the Feast of Our Lady of Guadalupe?

____

8. What does *Feliz Navidad* mean?

____

9. What Christmas flower comes from Mexico?

____

10. What is the most important festival in Mexico?

____

11. What flower did the Aztecs believe was sacred to the dead?

____

12. Where do families gather for the candlelight vigil?

____

Name ______________________________ Date ____________________

Make a Piñata

The piñata is a favorite part of most Mexican fiestas. Follow the instructions below to make your own piñata.

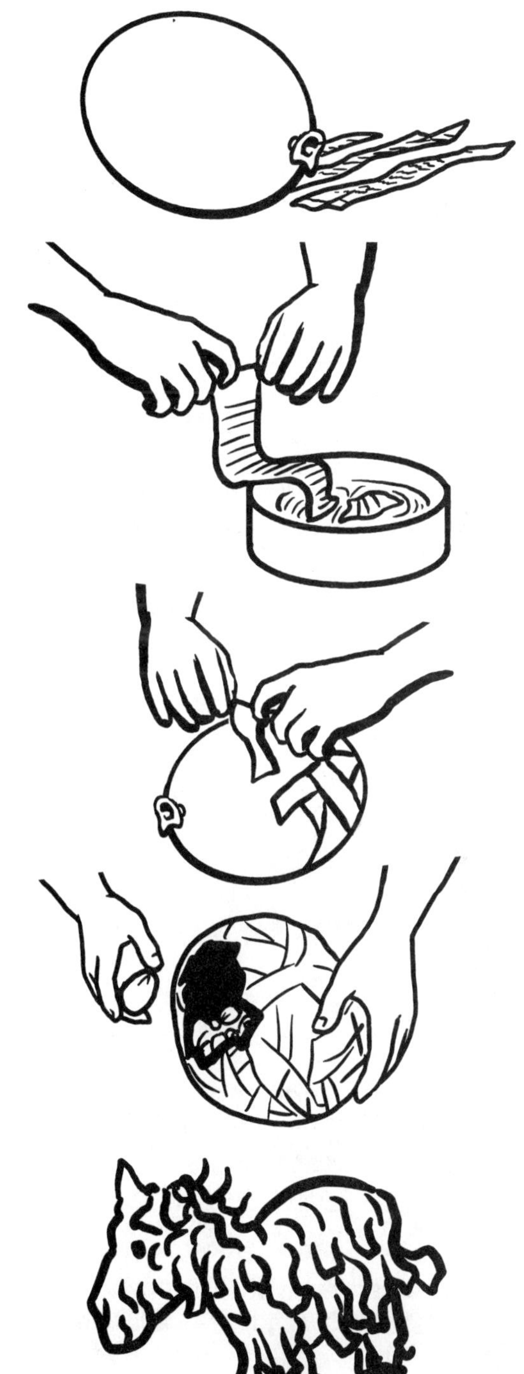

1. Inflate and tie the end of an oval or round balloon. The balloon should be at least 10 inches in diameter. Tear several strips of newspaper about one inch wide and one foot long.
2. Dip the newspaper strips into a watery paste or glue. Place the strips of paper onto the balloon. Apply four layers of paper around the balloon. Alternate the direction of the layers. Leave an opening of about two square inches near the stem of the balloon. Let dry for about three days.
3. After the paper is thoroughly dry, pop the balloon. Put candy and other prizes through the opening you left near the balloon's stem. Cover the opening with layers of newspaper dipped in glue. Let the opening dry.
4. You may now decorate the piñata. You may paint the piñata with tempera paint or cover it with colorful tissue paper. You may create an animal piñata by attaching a head, feet, and tail made of colored construction paper.

You are now ready to use your piñata at a party. Remember to be careful when swinging the stick to break the piñata. Everyone other than the blindfolded person should stay far enough away to avoid being accidentally hit by the stick.

Name ______________________________ Date ____________________

Crossword Puzzle

Use the clues below to complete the puzzle. You can find the words in the narrative about fiestas.

ACROSS

1. Many fiestas happen near this type of building.
3. Traditional Mexican Christmas flower
4. Container filled with candy and toys
5. The Aztecs believed this flower was sacred to the dead.
8. "Merry Christmas" in Spanish (two words)
11. The ______ of Our Lady of Guadalupe is an important fiesta.
12. For one festival, the people bake this in human forms and skull shapes.
13. The church of the Festival of the Virgin Mary is the ______ of the Virgin.
14. This and dancing are important parts of fiestas.

DOWN

2. Most fiestas observe this type of holiday.
3. The main Christmas celebration
6. *Muertitos chicos* is celebrated in this month.
7. This somber celebration honors the souls of the dead (four words).
9. The Feast of Our Lady of Guadalupe is held in this month.
10. Another word for fiesta (in English)

MEXICAN FOOD

Mexican food has increased in popularity throughout the United States. The number of Mexican restaurants and the items in grocery stores increases each year.

Mexican food includes native Indian foods, as well as foods with Spanish and some French influence.

Corn or maize has always been the main ingredient in Mexican cooking. Corn or wheat tortillas form the basis for most main dishes. Corn is also the basis of *atole,* a popular Mexican drink.

Other native ingredients, in addition to corn, include: tomatoes, potatoes, chocolate, pineapple, coconuts, papayas, turkey, vanilla, squash, beans, avocados, and chili peppers. The Spanish brought onions, garlic, beef, pork, chicken, and cheese from their homeland. The French influence, from the time of the Emperor Maximilian, includes breads and pastries.

A **tortilla** is made of corn or wheat (flour). It is rolled into a round, thin disk. The tortilla is fried or baked. Mexican meals often include rice or refried beans.

Some of the more common Mexican foods are:

Tacos—A tortilla filled with spiced meat, tomatoes, lettuce, and a chili sauce; this is perhaps the most famous Mexican food

Enchiladas—A tortilla filled with meat and cheese, baked, and then covered with a sauce

Tamales—Cornmeal dough tortilla, filled with meat and chili sauce, wrapped in corn husks, and steamed

Quesadillas—Grilled or fried tortillas with meat, cheese, potatoes, or chili

Chalupus - Tortillas fried and topped with meat, beans, chilies, tomatoes, and onions

Guacamole—A creamy mixture made from avocados; it is used as a dip or filling

Salsa—A sauce, sometimes spicy, made from tomatoes, onions, and chilies

Favorite traditional Mexican drinks include atole, hot chocolate, and coffee. Atole is made by boiling corn dough in water. Chocolate was popular with the Indians long before Columbus came to the Americas. Mexicans usually drink coffee after a meal. They seldom drink it on an empty stomach.

Tex-Mex is the name of food developed in Texas with a Mexican influence. Chili and chili con carne are Tex-Mex, not Mexican foods. If someone asked for a bowl of chili in Mexico, he or she might be served a bowl of chili peppers.

Name ______________________________ Date ____________________

Questions for Consideration

1.–3. What three cultures influenced Mexican food?

____

____

4. What is the main ingredient in Mexican cooking?

____

5. What is atole?

____

____

6. What is a tortilla?

____

____

7. What two types of tortillas are there? (two types of ingredients)

____

8. What is the main ingredient in guacamole?

____

9. What is salsa?

____

____

10. What drink was popular with the Indians before Columbus arrived?

____

11. Where was Tex-Mex food developed?

____

12. The narration mentioned what example of Tex-Mex food?

____

Name ______________________________ Date ____________________

Which Does Not Belong?

One word in each list below does not belong with the others. Circle the word in each group that is different. Tell why it is different on the line below each word group.

1. Beans Chocolate Corn Pastries

____

2. Cheese Onions Pork Turkey

____

3. Enchiladas Guacamole Tacos Tamales

____

4. France Native Indian Spain United States

____

5. Atole Chocolate Coffee Salsa

____

Matching

Match the food in the first column with the original source in the second column.

_____	1. Bread	A. Native Indian
_____	2. Tomatoes	B. Spanish
_____	3. Onions	C. French
_____	4. Beef	D. Tex-Mex
_____	5. Chocolate	
_____	6. Pastries	
_____	7. Cheese	
_____	8. Corn or maize	
_____	9. Chili con carne	
_____	10. Avocado	

Name ______________________________ Date ____________________

A Mexican Feast

Having a Mexican feast can be fun. Many grocery stores and supermarkets have Mexican foods available. Many cookbooks now contain recipes for the more common Mexican dishes. Below is a possible menu for a Mexican feast.

Appetizer: Salsa or guacamole and corn chips or tortilla chips

Main course: Any of the following, or a combination: tacos, enchiladas, tamales, quesadillas, chalupus
Served with rice or refried beans

Desert: Mexican fruit mix

Beverage: Chocolate milk or hot chocolate

Guacamole

Ingredients:
2 ripe avocados
2 chopped tomatoes (or one small can)
$\frac{1}{2}$ small onion chopped
2 Tbs. olive oil
pinch of salt and pepper
1 Tbs. lemon juice
pinch of chili pepper (optional)

1. Cut the avocado in half, remove the seed and skin.
2. Put all ingredients in blender, or mix thoroughly with a fork until mixture is smooth.

Refried Beans

Ingredients:
1 14-oz. can of kidney beans
1 medium onion
1 clove garlic
pinch of salt
2 Tbs. margarine
$\frac{1}{4}$ cup grated cheese

1. Peel and chop onion, crush garlic.
2. Fry onions and garlic in margarine until soft and brown.
3. Put mashed, drained beans into pan. Cook until hot.

Tomato Salsa

Ingredients:
2 tomatoes, peeled
1 small onion
pinch of salt and pepper
1 tsp. chili powder (optional)
pinch sugar

1. Chop the tomatoes and onions into small pieces.
2. Mix all ingredients together.

Mexican Fruit Mix

Ingredients:
apples
bananas
papayas
peaches
pineapples
1 tsp. cinnamon
1 small can frozen lemonade
chopped coconut

1. Cut fruit into bite-sized pieces.
2. Make a sauce by combining 1 tsp. cinnamon with 1 small can of frozen lemonade.
3. Cover fruit with sauce and top with chopped coconut.
4. Serve chilled.

MUSIC

The ancient native Indian tribes brought the first music into Mexico as early as 1500 B.C. They made instruments out of bone, wood, animal hides, and baked clay. Their instruments included whistles, flutes, drums, conch shells (as horns), drums, and other percussion instruments.

The Spanish and other Europeans brought music from their home lands. The early Spanish missionaries tried to suppress the Indian culture and its music, but much of the music that became what we know as Mexican is a blend of the two cultures.

The *mariachi* band is a familiar sight and sound throughout the country. The original mariachis were Indian musicians hired by Spanish men to serenade their girlfriends. The word *mariachi* may come from the French word *mariage* (marriage) because the bands often played at weddings.

The band members wear decorated jackets and ruffled shirts. They usually wear sombreros (wide brimmed hats). Early mariachi bands used stringed instruments, including violins, guitars, mandolins, and double basses. Later, the bands added brass instruments. Today, mariachi bands have three to 12 or more musicians. The typical band has six to eight members. Each mariachi band has a leader, a bass player, and two or more players of the violin, mandolin, guitar, and brass horn, usually trumpet.

Nortena is another popular Mexican music group. They are sometimes called *rancheros.* Europeans brought popular ballads with waltzes and polkas with them in the mid-nineteenth century. These styles blended with Indian music to form nortena. Ranch hands often sang nortena at the end of their work day.

Nortena bands usually have three members. The leader of the group, who is the singer, often plays a rhythm on a wood block with drumsticks. Other members include an accordionist and guitarist.

The most famous nortena song is *"La Cucaracha"* (the cockroach). Pancho Villa's soldiers sang *"La Cucaracha"* in the early part of the twentieth century.

The Spanish introduced the guitar into Mexico. It became an important and popular instrument. Other popular Mexican instruments include the marimba and the maracas.

The marimba is a percussion instrument made of a row of wood blocks on a bench-like frame. Each block has a pipe or box suspended below it. When the player strikes the wood block with a drumstick, the pipe or box resonates the sound.

Maracas are rattle-like instruments. Indians made rattles out of dried gourds. When they shook the gourd, the seeds made the sound. Modern maracas are hollowed wood, filled with dried beans. They have attached handles for easier use.

Modern Mexicans enjoy American and European popular music. In recent years, Mexican music is increasing in popularity in the United States.

Name ______________________________ Date ________________

Questions for Consideration

1.–2. What two cultures are blended into what we know as Mexican music?

3. What French word meant marriage?

4. What is a *sombrero?*

5. Today, how many players does a typical mariachi band have?

6. What is a *nortena?*

7. What is another name for nortena?

8. What famous Mexican folk song did Villa's soldiers sing?

9. What instrument did the Spanish introduce into Mexico?

10. What is the name of the percussion instrument made of rows of wooden blocks with boxes or pipes suspended below each block?

11. What did Indians use for a musical instrument that are now called maracas?

Name ______________________________ Date ____________________

Building Your Musical Vocabulary

You are familiar with many of the terms used in the narrative about Mexico's music. Others may be new to you. Using a dictionary, write out the exact meaning of the following terms.

1. Percussion: ____

2. Mariachi: ____

3. Serenade: ____

4. Mandolin: ____

5. Nortena: ____

6. Ballad: ____

7. Maracas: ____

Name ______________________________ Date ________________

Listening Activity

Mexican music has its own special sound. If you can locate a record, tape, or CD of some genuine Mexican music, listen to it.

1. What special things do you notice about the music?

____

____

2. What, if anything, do you like about Mexican music?

____

____

3. What, if anything, do you NOT like about Mexican music?

____

____

Match the Instrument

Match the instrument in the first column with its type in the second column. You may use a dictionary to help you.

_____ 1. Guitar

_____ 2. Trumpet

_____ 3. Marimba

_____ 4. Maracas

_____ 5. Violin

_____ 6. Drums

_____ 7. Conch shell

_____ 8. Mandolin

_____ 9. Bass

_____ 10. Flute

A. Wind

B. Percussion

C. String

THE ARTS

Some buildings in Mexico City feature traditional designs.

Many artists refer to Mexico as the "land of dazzling colors." Bright, vivid colors have been part of Mexico's arts and crafts since the time of the ancient Indian tribes.

Mexico has three major artistic eras: the native Indian, Spanish colonial, and the Revolution that led to Modern Art.

The major Indian cultures include the Olmec, Mayan, and Aztec. The designs and patterns of these tribes still influence Mexican artists.

Little remains of the Olmec civilization, other than some architectural ruins and carved-stone sculptures.

The Mayans were excellent weavers. Unfortunately, nothing remains of Mayan cloth, feather, or basket weaving. We know of their beautiful, brightly colored work from paintings remaining from the period. Many examples of Mayan pottery, sculpture, and painting remain.

Wonderful examples of Aztec architecture and sculpture still exist. Many examples of Aztec pottery and metal work are museum treasures today. The Aztecs were famous for their beautiful gold jewelry.

The Spanish influence is still obvious in Mexico. Examples of Spanish architecture, especially churches and missions, are national treasures. Spanish architecture often includes white buildings with red-tile roofs and small window openings. Spanish influence is also important in Mexican music.

Modern Mexican art dates from the Revolution of 1910. Large murals became the major contribution of Mexican artists to international modern art. The colorful murals of Diego Rivera and David Alfaro Siqueiros depict scenes from the Mexican revolution. They later dealt with themes of class struggles and social and political themes. Native Indian art influenced Rivera, who is perhaps Mexico's most famous artist.

Other noted artists include José Clemente Orozco, David Alfaro Siqueiros, Rufino Tamayo, and Juan O'Gorman.

Mexico has many important writers. Octavio Paz is a major poet, critic, and analyst. He won the Nobel Prize for Literature in 1990. Samuel Ramos is an important philosopher, specializing in man and culture in Mexico. Novelists include Carlos Fuentes, Gustavo Sainz, and Juan José Arreolas. Rodolfo Usigli remains Mexico's major playwright.

Major Mexican composers include Carlos Chávez and Silvestre Revueltas.

Many Mexican artists and craftsmen continue production of ancient, traditional crafts, including pottery and weaving. Others prefer to work with modern themes, techniques, and materials.

The Mexican government generously supports the arts. It sponsors the National Institute of Fine Arts. Its programs include the National Symphony, the Ballet Folklorico, and the Modern and Classical Ballet. The government also supports several internationally famous museums.

Name ______________________________ Date ____________________

Questions for Consideration

1. What phrase do many artists use when referring to Mexico?

____

2.–4. What are the three major eras of Mexican art?

____

____

____

5. Of what major Mayan art do we not have any remaining examples?

____

6. The Aztecs were noted for what kind of jewelry?

____

7.–8. In what two types of art did the Spanish influence become important in Mexico?

____

____

9. When did the Modern Art movement begin?

____

10. Who is considered to be Mexico's most famous artist?

____

11. What Mexican won the Nobel Prize for Literature?

____

12. Name a famous Mexican composer.

____

13. What is the name of the main government arts organization?

____

Name ______________________________ Date ____________________

Matching

Match the items in the first column with the correct response in the second column.

_____	1. Usigli	A. Poet
_____	2. Paz	B. Painter
_____	3. Rivera (Diego)	C. Composer
_____	4. Chávez	D. Philosopher
_____	5. Siqueiros	E. Playwright
_____	6. Revueltas	F. Novelist
_____	7. Fuentes	
_____	8. Sainz	
_____	9. Orozco	
_____	10. Ramos	

Word Scramble

Unscramble the following groups of letters to form words dealing with art. Then give a brief description of each word.

1. TASRFC ______________________________
2. NESDIG ______________________________
3. TANSPERT ______________________________
4. TRUEPULSC ______________________________
5. VANIGEW ______________________________
6. UCRIHTACETRE ______________________________
7. YLEJREW ______________________________
8. GARPHTLIYW ______________________________
9. SIMUC ______________________________
10. TORETYP ______________________________

Name ______________________________ Date ____________________

Make an Ojo de Dios

The Ojo de Dios (Eye of God) is a popular Mexican ornament made for festivals. Mexican and Central American Indians have made this decoration for hundreds of years. It is a diamond shape. The center diamond represents the eye of God. The outer diamonds represent light and wisdom coming from the eye.

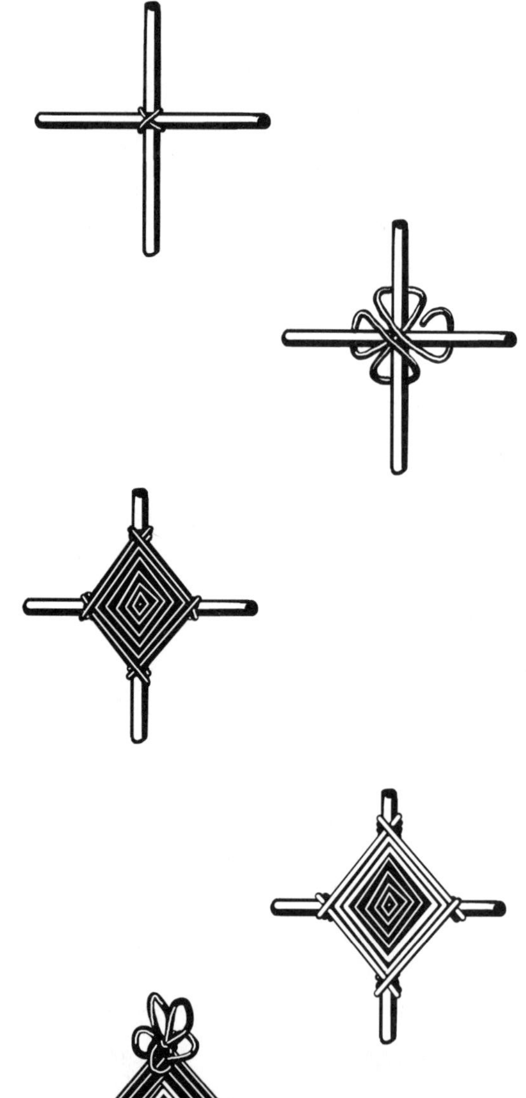

1. Make a cross out of two smooth sticks. The four parts of the cross should be even. Using a square knot, tie the two sticks together with a piece of yarn.
2. Start winding the yarn around the sticks, looping it around each part of the stick. As you continue winding the yarn around the stick, lay each yarn next to the yarn before it. The yarn should make flat rows.
3. After making several rows, change the color of the yarn. Put the end of the first color yarn at the back of one of the sticks. Wrap two loops of the second yarn around it to hold it in place. Change colors as often as you like.
4. Stop winding the yarn a little before you get to the end of the stick. Tie off the end of the last yarn used. Decorate the ends of the sticks with tassels or pompoms.

The Ojo de Dios makes a colorful ornament. You can make many of different sizes and they make excellent Christmas tree ornaments.

DIEGO RIVERA

(1886–1957)

This work by Diego Rivera depicts the ancient Aztec market at Tlatelolco.

Diego Rivera is Mexico's most famous artist. Rivera achieved international fame for his huge murals painted for public buildings. He also created many smaller paintings and graphics.

He was born on December 8, 1886, in Guanajuato. Both of his parents were teachers. They realized his talents early and encouraged his work.

He was drawing at the age of two. By the age of nine, he began to take lessons. He studied art at the age of 10 at the Academy of San Carlos in Mexico City.

In 1907, Rivera won a scholarship to study in Europe. He studied in Spain for a while. He soon moved to Paris where he met many of the leaders of the new Modern Art movement. The Revolution of 1910 occurred while Rivera lived in Paris.

Rivera returned to Mexico in 1921. He painted his first important mural for the University of Mexico. His early themes came from pre-Columbian art. Later his major themes were from Mexican history and the revolution.

Most art historians consider the fresco on the walls and ceiling of a chapel to be his masterpiece. The chapel is now part of an agricultural school near Mexico City.

Other important works include the mural *History of Cuernavaca and Morelos* in the Palace of Cortés in Cuernavaca. The *History of Mexico* is at the National Palace in Mexico City.

Between 1930 and 1934, he painted several murals in the United States. He painted *Allegory of California* for the Pacific Stock Exchange in San Francisco, *Making of a Fresco, Showing the Building of a City* in the San Francisco Art Institute, and *Detroit Industry* for the Detroit Institute of the Arts.

In 1933, he began *Man at the Crossroads* for the Rockefeller Center in New York City. It caused a controversy because it included a portrait of the communist leader, Lenin. He never finished the mural, and the owners destroyed it within a year. Rivera's last work in the United States during this period was a series of 21 political panels called *Portrait of America*. Only eight panels survive.

Rivera returned to Mexico in 1934. From 1937 to 1942, he received no commissions in Mexico and did several smaller paintings and portraits. During this time, he had one commission in the United States. It was *Pan-American Unity* for the World's Fair in San Francisco. After 1942, he resumed painting murals.

Rivera died in Mexico City on November 25, 1957.

Name ______________________________ Date ____________________

Questions for Consideration

1. What type of art made Diego Rivera famous?

2. When was Rivera born?

3. What was the occupation of Rivera's parents?

4. How old was Rivera when he began drawing?

5. What important event happened to Rivera in 1907?

6. When did Rivera return to Mexico?

7. What was the source of themes for Rivera's early work?

8. What is the name of Rivera's mural for the National Palace in Mexico City?

9. What was the name of Rivera's mural that was destroyed because of a controversy?

10. How many panels of *Portrait of America* survive?

11. For what event did Rivera paint *Pan-American Unity?*

12. Where did Rivera die?

Name ______________________________ Date ____________________

Building Your Art Vocabulary

You are familiar with many of the terms used in the narrative about Diego Rivera and his art. Others may be new to you. Using a dictionary, write out the exact meaning of the following terms.

1. Mural: ____

2. Theme: ____

3. Fresco: ____

4. Allegory: ____

5. Institute: ____

6. Commission: ____

7. Portrait: ____

Art Art Activity

If possible, look at pictures of Diego Rivera's murals in a book or encyclopedia. Notice his style and use of colors. Also notice the subjects of his work. On a large piece of paper, draw and color or paint your own mural in the same style as Rivera.

Answer Keys

INTRODUCTION—QUESTIONS (page 5)

1. The United Mexican States
2. Los Estados Unidos Mexicanos
3. 1,933 miles

4.–5. Guatemala, Belize

6.–7. Indian and Spanish

8. Mexico City

9.–10. (Two of the following) Cancun, Acapulco, Mazatlan, Puerto Vallarta, Veracruz

11.–12. (Two of the following) population, crime, pollution, drugs

13. oil
14. September 16

INTRODUCTION—WHICH DOES NOT BELONG (page 6)

1. Panama: does not border Mexico
2. Spanish: is not an Indian culture
3. Mexico City: is not a resort destination
4. onions: not listed as a major crop
5. pizza: is not a Mexican food

INTRODUCTION—LIST THE CONTRASTS (page 6)

1. Indian and Spanish
2. Indian cities, Spanish churches, skyscrapers
3. (Two of the following) mountains, plateaus, deserts, beaches, jungles
4. (Two of the following) dry (deserts), wetlands (jungles)

INTRODUCTION—MATCHING (page 7)

1. B	6. D	11. D
2. E	7. A	12. B
3. A	8. F	13. E
4. C	9. C	14. F
5. B	10. E	15. D

GEOGRAPHY—QUESTIONS (page 9)

1. The United States

2.–3. Guatemala, Belize

4. Pacific

5.–6. Gulf of Mexico, Bay of Campeche

7. funnel or triangular
8. Sierra Madre
9. Citlaltépetl or Orizaba Volcano

10.–11. Yucatan, Baja California

12. Rio Grande (Rio Bravo del Norte)
13. Chapala

14.–15. earthquakes, volcanoes

GEOGRAPHY—MAP EXERCISE (page 10)

Teacher check map.

GEOGRAPHY—VOCABULARY (page 11)

Answers will vary.

MEXICO'S PEOPLE—QUESTIONS (page 13)

1.–2. Spanish, Indian

3. bullfighting
4. a person with a mix of European and native Indian heritage
5. about one third
6. Roman Catholic
7. Virgin of Guadalupe

8.–10. Mexico City, Guadalajara, Monterrey

11. six years
12. Spanish
13. Aztec native language
14. over 60

THE PEOPLE—UNDERSTANDING PIE GRAPHS (page 14)

1. 44,000,000
2. 26,400,000
3. 13,200,000
4. 4,400,000

5. 42,500,000,000
6. 8,500,000,000
7. 42,500,000,000
8. 17,000,000,000

THE PEOPLE—CROSSWORD PUZZLE (page 15)

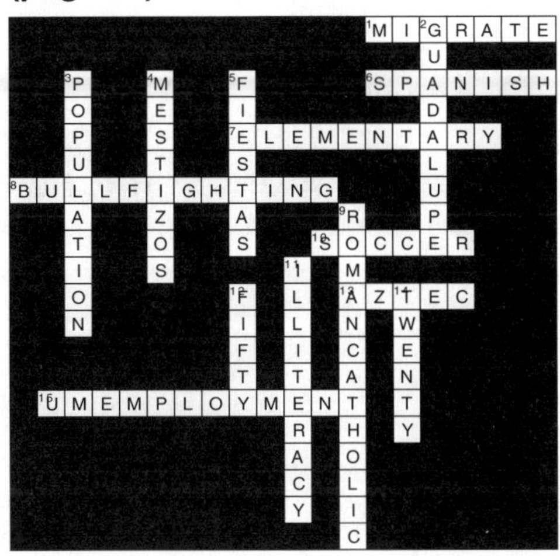

EARLY CIVILIZATIONS—QUESTIONS (page 17)

1. About 8000 B.C.
2. Bering Strait
3. 2000–1000 B.C.
4. Olmec
5. 700–400 B.C.
6.–7. San Lorenzo and La Venta
8. heads
9. Altiplano
10. 200 B.C.–A.D. 600
11. Teotihuacán
12. Pyramid of the Sun
13. A.D. 750
14. It is still a mystery.

EARLY CIVILIZATIONS—USING A TIME LINE (page 18)

1. 8,705 years
2. 6,000 years
3. 300 years
4. 200 years
5. 300 years

EARLY CIVILIZATIONS—A POSSIBLE JOURNEY (page 19)

The route is left up to the imagination.
Dates to be labeled are:
Beginning: 8000 B.C.
Entered U.S.: anything after 8000 B.C. and before 2000 B.C.
Reached Mexico: 2000–1000 B.C.
Teotihuacán burned: A.D. 750

THE MAYAS - QUESTIONS (page 21)

1. Olmec
2. 2500 B.C.–A.D. 1500s
3. Yucatan
4.–5. Copán and Chichén Itzá
6. Pyramid of Kukulcan
7. maize
8. picture symbols
9. zero
10. 18
11. halach uinic
12. human
13. We do not know.
14. Christopher Columbus

THE MAYAS—FACT OR OPINION (page 22)

1. F
2. F
3. O
4. F
5. O
6. O
7. O
8. F
9. O
10. F

THE MAYAS—MAKING COMPARISONS (page 23)

1. Mayas borrowed from the Olmecs.
2. The Pyramid of Kukulcan is the most famous Mayan structure.
3. They also had advanced agriculture.
4. They used glyphs (picture symbols).
5. They also made paper and books.
6. They used a zero.
7. They believed in many gods.
8. They also had a calendar with 365 days.
9. Their calendar had 18 months.
10. Their calendar had 20 days in each month.

THE AZTECS—QUESTIONS (page 25)

1. Tenochtitlan
2. Mexico City
3. picture
4. clan
5. 20
6. Montezuma I
7. the family

8. small island made in lake or swamp
9. over 60
10. human sacrifice
11.–12. lunar and solar
13. 1519
14. 1521

THE AZTECS—WHICH DOES NOT BELONG (page 26)

1. Mexico City - not an Aztec city
2. cabbage - not a major Aztec food or not an Aztec word
3. mass media - not used by Aztecs
4. Olmec - not an Aztec word
5. made communes - not made by Aztecs or not part of Aztec agriculture

THE AZTECS—MATCHING (page 26)

1. E
2. I
3. A
4. J
5. B
6. C
7. H
8. D
9. G
10. F

THE AZTECS—WORD SCRAMBLE (page 27)

1. Aztec
2. Tenochtitlan
3. tomato
4. chocolate
5. calpolli
6. Montezuma
7. chinampas
8. human sacrifice
9. calendars
10. Cortés

THE SPANISH—QUESTIONS (page 29)

1. 1517
2. Cortés
3. New Spain
4. over 300,000
5. born in Spain then settled in Mexico
6. full Spanish descent, born in Mexico
7. mixed Spanish and Indian heritage
8. the Franciscans
9. in the 17th century
10. Bourbon
11. Hidalgo y Costilla
12. September 27, 1821

THE SPANISH—ARRANGE IN CHRONOLOGICAL ORDER (page 30)

1. 6
2. 8
3. 10
4. 5
5. 1
6. 9
7. 2
8. 4
9. 7
10. 3

THE SPANISH—CROSSWORD PUZZLE (page 31)

CORTÉS AND MONTEZUMA—QUESTIONS (page 33)

1. 1519
2. 1521 or three years later
3. 1502
4. a god, or Quetzalcoatl
5. buy him off, keep him out of the capital
6. November 8, 1519
7. It was like a dream.
8. made him a prisoner
9. threw stones at him
10. 1521
11. Seville, Spain
12. Mexico

INDEPENDENCE—QUESTIONS (page 37)

1. He led the first major rebellion against the Spanish.
2. Augustin de Iturbide
3. Guadalupe Victoria
4. Santa Anna
5. battle of the Alamo
6. Mexican War (also Texas war for independence)
7. Maximilian
8. court-martialed and executed
9. Porfirio Diaz

10.–11. resented monopoly of power, hated foreign control of industry

12.–13. copper, textiles

INDEPENDENCE—VOCABULARY (page 38)

Answers will vary

INDEPENDENCE—SEQUENCING (page 39)

9, 3, 4, 10, 5, 8, 1, 6, 2, 7

INDEPENDENCE—FACT OR OPINION (page 39)

1. F
2. O
3. O
4. O
5. F
6. F
7. O
8. F
9. F
10. O

SANTA ANNA—QUESTIONS (page 41)

1. government official
2. Iturbide
3. 1833
4. San Antonio
5. the Alamo
6. Texas independence
7. his leg
8. Zachary Taylor

9.–10. Buena Vista and Cerro Gordo

11. treason
12. June 20, 1876

SANTA ANNA—MAP EXERCISE (page 42)

1. San Antonio
2. Cuba
3. Saint Thomas
4. Mexico City
5. Jamaica
6. Venezuela

AFTER REVOLUTION—QUESTIONS (page 45)

1. Francisco I. Madero
2. 15 months

3.–4. dissolved congress, arrested its members

5. Francisco (Pancho) Villa
6. Emiliano Zapata
7. Woodrow Wilson
8. Carranza
9. Northern Dynasty
10. Lázaro Cárdenas
11. placed it under Mexican government control

AFTER REVOLUTION—MEXICO'S PRESIDENTS (page 46)

1. 4 years
2. 6 years
3. Venustiano Carranza
4. Manuel Avila Camacho
5. Lázaro Cárdenas

PANCHO VILLA—QUESTIONS (page 49)

1. Robin Hood
2. an outlaw
3. Madero
4. Juárez
5. El Paso
6. Division del Norte
7. Woodrow Wilson
8. Celaya
9. murdered Americans
10. John J. Pershing
11. pardoned him
12. killed by his enemies

PANCHO VILLA—ARRANGE IN CHRONOLOGICAL ORDER (page 50)

1. D
2. F
3. B
4. H
5. J

6. A
7. G
8. E
9. I
10. C

MODERN MEXICO—QUESTIONS (page 53)

1. supplied raw materials
2. 50 percent higher
3. unemployment
4. 1958
5. oil
6. decline of oil prices
7. over $100 billion
8. earthquake
9. hurricane Gilbert

10.–11. drugs and illegal immigrants

12. North American Free Trade Agreement

MODERN MEXICO—USING A BAR GRAPH (page 54)

1. 25 million
2. 1980
3. It doubled.
4. 1940s (1940–1950)
5. 1970s (1970–1980)

MEXICO CITY—QUESTIONS (page 57)

1. Ciudad de México
2. 10 million
3. 18 million
4. Tenochtitlán
5. its high elevation
6. 60 percent
7. because of pollution
8. an earthquake

9.–12. any 4 of the following: National Cathedral, Aztec plaza, largest market, Maximilian's castle, Plaza México, National Museum of History, Museum of Anthropology, art galleries

13. the National University

MEXICO CITY—GOOD AND BAD (page 58)

Answers will vary, Possible responses:
Good: climate, contrasts, list of tourist attractions
Bad: population, pollution, earthquakes, slums, crime

MEXICO CITY—CROSSWORD PUZZLE (page 59)

MEXICO'S CITIES—QUESTIONS (page 61)

1.–4. Tijuana, Mexicali, Juárez, Nogales

5. Mazatlán
6. Monterrey
7. Guadalajara
8. Teotihuacán
9. Acapulco
10. Cancún
11. Puerto Vallarta
12. Veracruz
13. Cozumel
14. Cancùn

MEXICO'S CITIES—MAP EXERCISE (page 62)

1. Tijuana
2. Juárez
3. Monterrey
4. Mexico City
5. Veracruz
6. Cancún
7. Mazatlán
8. Puerto Vallarta
9. Guadalajara
10. Acapulco
11. Cozumel

MEXICO'S CITIES—PLANNING A TRIP (page 63)

1.–5. Acapulco, Cancùn, Cozumel, Puerto Vallarta, Mazatlán

6.–9. Tijuana, Mexicali, Juárez, Nogales

10.–11. Teotihuacán, Cancùn

12. Monterrey
13.–14. Veracruz, Guadalajara

MEXICO'S GOVERNMENT—QUESTIONS (page 65)

1. the Constitution of 1917
2. 31
3. one-house
4. over 2,400
5.–7. executive, legislative and judicial
8. six years
9.–10. Senate and Chamber of Deputies
11. Supreme Court of Justice
12. Institutional Revolutionary Party

MEXICO'S GOVERNMENT—MAKING COMPARISONS (page 66)

1. is a federal republic
2. has 31 states
3. one house legislature
4. the same (three branches: executive, legislative, judicial)
5. term is six years
6. may serve only one term
7. does not have vice president
8. Senate has 64 members
9. Chamber of Deputies has 500 members
10. may only serve one term in a row

FIESTA—QUESTIONS (page 70)

1. celebrations
2. Mexico
3. one or two days
4. around the church or in the main plaza
5. colorful container filled with candy and toys
6. Mexico City
7. December 12
8. Merry Christmas
9. poinsettia
10. Day of the Dead
11. marigold
12. in town cemetery or at graves of relatives

FIESTA—CROSSWORD (page 72)

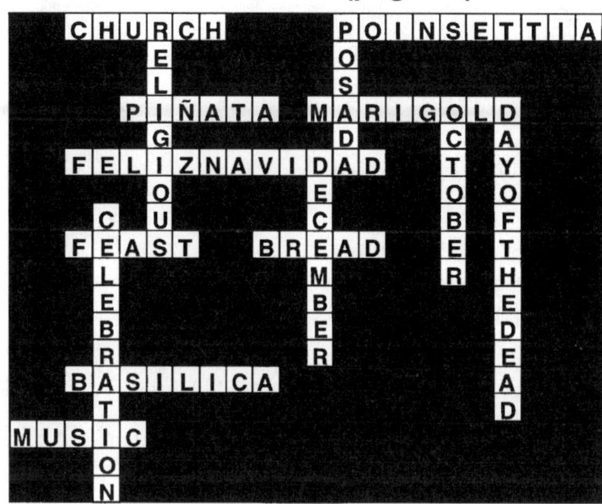

MEXICAN FOOD—QUESTIONS (page 74)

1.–3. Indian, Spanish, French
4. corn
5. drink made from corn
6. round, thin disk
7. corn, wheat (flour)
8. avocado
9. a sauce
10. hot chocolate
11. Texas
12. chili or chili con carne

MEXICAN FOOD—WHICH DOES NOT BELONG (page 75)

1. pastries - not a native Indian food
2. turkey - not brought over by Spanish
3. Guacamole - does not contain a tortilla
4. United States - did not influence Mexican food
5. Salsa - is not a beverage

MEXICAN FOOD—MATCHING (page 75)

1. C
2. A
3. B
4. B
5. A
6. C
7. B
8. A
9. D
10. A

MUSIC—QUESTIONS (page 78)

1.–2. Indian and Spanish
3. mariage (only one "r")
4. wide-brimmed hat
5. six to eight
6. popular music group
7. ranchero
8. "La Cucaracha"
9. guitar
10. marimba
11. dried gourds

MUSIC—MATCHING (page 80)

1. C
2. A
3. B
4. B
5. C
6. B
7. A
8. C
9. C
10. A

THE ARTS—QUESTIONS (page 82)

1. "land of dazzling colors"
2.–4. native Indian, Spanish colonial, Revolution leading to Modern Art
5. weaving
6. gold
7.–8. architecture, music
9. with the revolution of 1910
10. Diego Rivera
11. Octavio Paz
12. Carlos Chávez or Silvestre Revueltas
13. National Institute of Fine Arts

THE ARTS—MATCHING (page 83)

1. E
2. A
3. B
4. C
5. B
6. C
7. F
8. F
9. B
10. D

THE ARTS—WORD SCRAMBLE (page 83)

1. crafts
2. design
3. patterns
4. sculpture
5. weaving
6. architecture
7. jewelry
8. playwright
9. music
10. pottery

RIVERA—QUESTIONS (page 86)

1. huge murals (painted for public buildings)
2. December 8, 1886
3. teachers
4. two
5. received scholarship to study in Europe
6. 1921
7. pre-Columbian art
8. *History of Mexico*
9. *Man at the Crossroads*
10. eight
11. San Francisco World's Fair
12. Mexico City